About the Author

Suzanne is the owner and manager of Sunny Brow Holistic Retreat and mother to three spirited young children. Her gift in life has been the vision and dedication to create a centre where people can come and stay on retreat, individually or as a group, to be nourished on a deep level, with whole foods, treatments and yoga, to learn and be inspired by a life closer to nature, body and soul.

She has always had a passion for healthy eating and holistic living, researching and reading avidly in this area, and her interest and purpose has been to understand what is best for the body and how to apply this. Making steps to heal on a nutritional and physical level also led her to healing on an emotional and spiritual level, and her practice and daily life now incorporate many elements to aid this journey. She does not only teach from study courses and theory, but works hard to live and breathe her beliefs.

Her degree in psychology, and enthusiasm for what makes us tick, was continued on a life changing course with the International Macrobiotic School, where she began learning holistic counselling, and healing using emotional patterns with the five elements. From this work, she has built her own practise and business offering macrobiotic consultations and cooking classes to assist in diet, emotional well-being and lifestyle.

In addition, she is a yoga teacher, trained since 2003, a Reiki Master, healing massage and crystals practitioner, a shamanic practitioner, and is also currently training in the All Nations sweat lodge. With an eclectic mix of healing practices, her life has become richer and fuller, with more understanding and happiness, and less health and emotional turbulence. She is now dedicated to continuing this journey for herself, her family and to also share this with the guests coming to stay at Sunny Brow.

www.sunnybrowfarm.co.uk

Suzanne Saunders

CONSCIOUS COOKERY

SEASONAL RECIPES AND INSPIRATIONS FROM SUNNY BROW HOLISTIC RETREAT

Photography: Kerttu Kruusla & Triin Reilson

Design: Kerttu Kruusla

AUSTIN MACAULEY PUBLISHERS™
LONDON • CAMBRIDGE • NEW YORK • SHARJAH

Copyright © Suzanne Saunders (2018)

ISBN 9781788235563 (Paperback)
ISBN 9781788235570 (Hardback)
ISBN 9781788235587 (E-Book)
www.austinmacauley.com

First Published (2018)
Austin Macauley Publishers™ Ltd
25 Canada Square
Canary Wharf
London
E14 5LQ

Dedication

I dedicate this book to Mother Earth, and to all those who care for her well-being and have gratitude for all she provides.

Acknowledgments

I want to give heartfelt thanks to all those who have supported my journey with this book; to those on my Seasonal Cookery Course who rode the book's first journey with me; to Triin and Kerttu for their loving support and wonderful creativity; to Marijke de Coninck and Oliver Cowmeadow for an inspiring course that helped, in part, to build the foundations of this book; and extra thanks to Oliver for his knowledge and support with the seasonal and elemental writings.

To the children for their ideas and enthusiasm for 'Mummy's cook book'; to my parents for their support and love; and last, but not least, to my husband Philip, who held and supported me whilst I flourished into the woman who was able to write this book, for his continued efforts at patience with me and for his unending love.

CONTENTS

I believe, and always have done, that 'we are what we eat'. The last 20 years for me has been about exploring this concept, educating myself, learning to cook fresh, healthy foods and becoming more fully conscious of what goes into my body. It's been a great journey of exploration and self-discovery that has also led to a deepening in many other areas of my life. I'm enthusiastic to share the riches to be found; to tell of a way that we can live a life that's more full and happy, with more energy, and better health and wellbeing. I feel more self aware, more empowered, and in control of my own life, and no longer victim to varying fads and diets, or chronic ill health.

This book is a fusion of the things I have connected with on this personal journey towards healthy living, nutritional awareness of our bodies' needs, wild foods and home grown harvests, macrobiotics and the five elements, extensively studied at the International Macrobiotic School in Totnes, and my love of connecting fully to each and every season. By connecting with the energies in and around us, to the energies of the seasons and to the ingredients that nature provides, we can open to a deeper connection, sensitivity and self care.

When we eat something, we are taking its energy into our bodies, it will have a nutritional, but also energetic, impact. To build an understanding and work with this can help to bring us back into balance, flow with greater ease in our individual lives, and gives us strength and vitality to be who we truly are. The seasonal sections in this book have been written, cooked and photographed in the right season to fully bring in the energy of each time of year. From seasonal awareness of the elements, we can begin to heal the body; we are nature, we are the elements, looking to what nature provides us, to the cycle of life; within each year and each day, we can become more in balance. As the cycle changes, we can link our awareness, and bodies, by the foods we eat and the cooking methods we choose, by the subtle wisdoms of nature and the wisdoms in our own hearts.

My main aim with this book, and with the cookery courses I run, is to inspire a healthy way of living that comes from the body and intuition, not just from the mind. Our journeys are all very individual; we are all unique. We must make food and life style choices that support our own lives, there is no one diet or one way that is right for all of us. This is a book to help the flow of your own creativity and intuition for holistic living that's right for you, and to also build a love of simple organic whole foods that suit your body. The purpose is for you to bring it into your home and kitchen, take bits and pieces, recipes, healing, inspiration, take what you need, and run with it to suit your own life.

SUNNY BROW FARM HOLISTIC RETREAT

Sunny Brow Farm is an old Cumbrian Farm near Ambleside that has had an eclectic history with vibrant and alternative owners, which have all added to Sunny Brow's interesting energy of nature, healing and connection to Mother Earth. Forming the essence of this energy is an ancient native woodland with stunning oaks, coppiced hazel, beautiful old hawthorns, a limestone beck, and old limestone quarry and kiln, and wild animals and birds, including hares, owls, bats, foxes, badgers, deer and buzzards.

We moved here and renovated Sunny Brow at a time when farming on the land had dwindled and the barns had been neglected for many years. Breathing life back into the land and buildings has been a great joy. It's been a journey of hard work and commitment, but it's been very worthwhile. With the old Cumbrian barns, using love and careful restoration, we have created beautiful accommodation, where people can come, stay to benefit from relaxing close to nature.

For me, living at Sunny Brow has been a journey into rediscovering a connection to nature. I have witnessed in myself a gradual shift to being far more connected to what is happening in nature, to the rhythm of the year, to the cycle of life, to edible plants on my doorstep, and the habitats and patterns of the wild animals and birds. This has linked well to my work and interest of understanding what is best for the body and how to apply it. My healing journey is on a nutritional and physical level and on an emotional and spiritual level, with practise and daily life now incorporating many elements to aid this journey. I do not only teach from study courses and theory, but work hard to live and breathe my beliefs. With an eclectic mix of healing practices, I feel my life has become richer and fuller, with more understanding and happiness, and less health and emotional turbulence.

Now an up and coming retreat centre, a place for people to come and stay, unfurl, and unfold, Sunny Brow is here to touch the hearts of many. My aim is that people can be nourished and nurtured, refreshed and revitalised that they can connect to nature, to Mother Earth, to what's real, and to see and open to the truth of themselves.

Guests can come and stay here with us on retreat, individually or as a group, to be nourished on a deep level, with whole foods, treatments and yoga. We run courses, workshops, cookery classes and a variety of organised retreats designed to heal mind and body, and open to a deepen connection to earth and soul. On our organised retreats, we always follow the energy of the work we are doing with the food we serve, it's an integral part of the retreats. Welcoming people to stay here at Sunny Brow is a true joy.

HOLISTIC LIVING & EATING

Holistic living and eating is an adventure, life becomes an adventure, a journey into one's self and beyond. I believe it is about discovering yourself and the truth of life, whatever that means for you, and coming into connection to this truth. I have always held in my heart the vision of a place like Sunny Brow and things in my life have led me to this point of birthing my dream into being. I believe this is possible for all our dreams. Supporting myself with connection to good foods and conscious awareness of what I am choosing to put in my body has been key to this unfolding.

The most profound thing I have found is that the more I walk this path, the deeper I am connected to my true self and Mother Earth. I have become more sensitive and feel drawn to take better care. On this journey, my awareness has expanded, I am learning to honour the Earth and what we have inherited, honouring our ancestors, and all that is around us in nature. I am learning to honour myself and I feel I am letting go of any arrogance and ultimately finding connection to a deeper love and intimacy, with myself, with friends, family, colleagues and strangers, to plants, animals, and our earth. What a great unfolding of love and joy, but always with ups and downs, a constantly unfolding journey. I am dedicated to continuing this journey for myself and my family, and to also share this with the guests coming to stay at Sunny Brow.

14

CONSCIOUS EATING

EATING WITH THE SEASONS

Seasons are great. I love them, and they felt perfect to create the chapters of this book. For me, to connect with nature is to connect with each season in turn, to honour and respect, and get insight and harmony from tuning in. The recipes I have created in each seasonal section are connected to what is available at that time of year and are also based on the energies that can give us an underlying support at each time of year.

Autumn is the beginning of the colder months, and then winter to follow can get colder and darker. It feels good to nourish ourselves with warm grounding foods, long cooked stews, baking vegetables and enjoying the root vegetables; in addition, kale and other dark greens can be a useful seasonal vegetable that provide minerals and also a good balancing uplifting energy.

In spring and summer, it is warmer and can be drier and brighter. Things growing include salads, fruits and lighter vegetables; we naturally look to these foods to support us in a warmer climate. It feels natural to eat salads and lighter cooked foods in the summer. It is beneficial for us, and the Earth, to eat what grows around us in our natural environment, at each time of year.

Each season holds the energy of an element; when I tune in, I can really feel this energy at each time of year. The elements form a cycle around from beginning to end. This cycle is within the whole of life; even each breath has a whole cycle with four parts: inhale, space, exhale, space. Each day is a cycle; morning is like spring, then comes midday like summer, and the afternoon is autumn and then night is like winter. Women flow through the seasons each month within their menstrual cycle: first part holds the energy of spring, then summer is ovulation, premenstrual is autumn and bleeding is winter.

A full cycle is balanced and whole. We are the elements; we flow with all of them in our body, we flow with the whole cycle. Eating with awareness of the elements is a great way to support our health and spiritual growth. Using this book, the recipes and inspirations will open a deeper awareness into the seasons and to eating in connection with the elements. Do be aware of balance; eating too much of a particular food and flavour, even in the right season, can be also disruptive. So keep interest and balance with variety, and a varying array of flavours and cooking styles on your plate in one meal, and through out the day. A full and balanced macrobiotic meal will include energy from all the elements, either from ingredients or cooking method.

EATING FOODS FROM MOTHER EARTH

Creating deep connection, balance and eating for vibrant energy comes from mainly eating foods close to Mother Earth's natural state. Look to reducing processed foods, and choose foods that are still full of life and vitality such as, whole grains, pulses and lentils, vegetables, sea vegetables, fresh and dried fruit, seeds, nuts, wild foods and fermented foods. As these foods are still 'alive' until they are cooked or prepared, it means this strong energy is there ready and waiting for us to benefit from. This book includes a variety of all these foods; there is a vast selection which helps to create interest, creativity and joy for our cooking and eating. Whole food eating is much more simple, yet the choice and wide range of grains, pulses, vegetables, seasonings available allows for a variety of energy and tastes that we can use to help ourselves flourish. Eating a wide variety also ensures that we get the all of the right nutrients from our food in a good balance.

Vegetables are brilliant, a super food. I eat as many as I can in a day. They are outrageously delicious, they contain phyto-oestrogens that keep our bodies balanced, they are moderately alkaline, and they contain heaps of vitamins and minerals that are beneficial to the body. With an array of flavours and energies to suit our need and mood, what better food could we use to nourish our bodies. Vegetables are very versatile, you can use them in soups, stews, stir-fries, salads they can be baked in the oven, steamed, and pickled. For deeper inspiration on their goodness, it's good to see they have an eclectic mix of different energies that we can tap into for maximum support.

Upward growing vegetables: kale, leafy greens, watercress, leeks, parsley, spring onions, celery and lettuces. These vegetables give us minerals and their energy uplifts us, which can be good for liver, gallbladder, and heart.

Grounded and rounded veggies: turnips, pumpkin, butternut squash, swede, cabbage, onions, beetroots. These give a soothing, centring and warming energy, good for our middle organs, stomach spleen, pancreas and womb in women. Great choices for grounded energy or receiving nourishment.

Downward growing: carrots, parsnips, radish, dandelion root, these help ground and give roots helping keep our energy centred and inwards, good if feeling scattered, disorganised, and/or needing to grow stronger roots in life; great to help the lungs and large intestines.

Sea vegetables: wakame, kombu, arame, dulse, nori; holding the energy of the sea and the essence of life, these vegetables give nourishment from many vitamins and minerals. Great for supporting the kidneys and bladder, and to restore vitality when feeling depleted and low in energy.

Whole grains,

which our ancestors would have eaten from wild grasses, are an amazing food essential for holistic health. Evidence from paleoanthropologists suggest that our diet consisted of a variety of plant foods, including starches. Starch granules from plants have been found on fossil teeth and stone tools, which suggests humans may have been gathering and eating grains for at least 100,000 years. Whole grains are fibrous and packed with minerals, vitamins and energy, including iron and calcium. The energy in a whole grain is very strong as it carries the energy of a new plant. They are good for physical and mental health, mental stability and spiritual connectedness. Great grains to start using are barley, whole oats, millet, corn on the cob, brown rice, and quinoa. See p.67 for ideas and cooking tips. Baked flour products are less recommended, grains that are ground and baked will give a much more contractive energy. This can be healthy when wholegrain and used in moderation, however, white flour products are highly processed and unhealthy.

Pulses,

including lentils, peas and beans, are edible seeds that grow in pods. They are a highly nutritious vegetarian protein packed with fibre, B vitamins, iron, zinc and potassium; they are low in fat and low in carbon footprint, and inexpensive to buy. They are also high in probiotics that help healthy bacteria to grow in the gut. Great choices for these include chickpeas, puy lentils, aduki beans, black beans, mung beans, red lentils, and green and yellow split peas. See p.38 for ideas and cooking tips.

Wild food

and foraging is becoming a big trend, and I can see why. It's a really great feeling to bring a bit of the wild into your kitchen.

It helps a connection to how things grow, of where different plants come from, and it has taught me a greater respect for food and food resources. Connecting to plants by foraging can help us to connect to their essence and our essence, and can promote health and wellbeing by being conscious and aware. I always make sure I pick and harvest with love and consciousness. On a serious note, please make sure you know exactly what you are harvesting before eating; my recommendation would be to join a wild food walk from a foraging expert.

Seeds and nuts are an essential part of our diet, they contain an array of nutrients to support our bodies. Seeds are high in fibre, vitamin E and monounsaturated fats, protein, minerals, zinc and other essential nutrients. Just a small quantity provides these essential fats, vitamins and minerals, for the heart, immune system and brain, supporting health and vitality. Great seeds are pumpkin, sunflower, sesame, flax and hemp seeds; great nuts are almonds, walnuts, pistachios, pecans, hazelnuts and peanuts. Here at Sunny Brow, we have hazel trees and it's rewarding and fun, although quite hard work to harvest our own.

Fermented foods are thankfully coming back into fashion. With the use of fridges and freezers, the need to ferment our food declined. But the health benefits are so good that it feels important that we carry on with this style of food preparation. Fermentation is a process of lactofermentation where the natural bacteria feed on the sugar and starch in the food and lactic acid is created. This process preserves the food, but also creates beneficial enzymes, b-vitamins, Omega-3 fatty acids, and various strains of probiotics; the nutrients, including vitamin C, in the vegetables are also actually increased by the fermentation process. Good fermented products to start including in the diet are pickled vegetables, kimchi, tempeh, miso, shoyu and sauerkraut.

THE RIGHT KIND OF SWEETNESS

I believe, as humans, we all need sweetness in our lives, to one degree or another. It is stimulating, fun, and holds the energy of love, mother's care and nurture; to cut it out and remove it from our lives is crazy, and probably impossible. However, to become aware of its energy, and our need for it, is important so we can know when and how to bring it into our lives in the right way.

White sugar expands and stimulates us, and has an initial upward energy in the body. It is understandable that it is popular and addictive, especially in our hectic lives rushing from here and there. However, as sugar is an incredibly refined processed product, it is very extreme and makes a massive impact, eventually producing a 'crash'. It also actually robs the body of vitamins and minerals, I call it negative nutrition. Blood sugar imbalance, mood swings, acidic blood, addiction, inflammation of body joints and muscles, and scattered thinking can all be results of refined white sugar. Unconsciously eating high sugar products is clearly doing us more harm than good.

Becoming more conscious of what, and when, we eat 'sweetness' is the key to beating the sugar addictions. Are you grabbing sugar or alcohol when you get back from a hard days work? Are you needing more rest and choosing sweet options to keep going? Are you looking for ways to escape? Notice if it is the body and mind needing a balance, could there be a different option? Work to bring in some calmer and natural ways of sweetness. Natural sweetness can come from sugar alternatives such barley malt, rice syrup, and sometimes maple syrup and honey; using dried and fresh fruits and fruit juices is also a more balanced and healthy option. Vegetables are a great way to bring in a natural sweetness that will also help to combat sugar cravings. The more you come away from refined sugar, the more your taste buds will enjoy natural sweet flavours. In fact, in time, sugary things become unpleasantly sweet, and you also start to notice the negative impact on the body more.

The other thing to help sugar cravings is to assess your lifestyle balance. Look to reducing stress, perhaps working less long hours and getting more rest when it's needed. Choosing yoga and calm breathing techniques to relax and getting support from friends, or massage and alternative therapies can all really help. All these techniques will help achieve a better overall balance and reduce the need for the very extreme sugar options to keep us going when it's time to stop.

INTUITIVE AND MINDFUL EATING

Eat calmly, chew well and enjoy for food. Creating a good energy around food will ensure enjoyment of your meal times and you are, therefore, more likely to continue with any new changes. Cook and eat in a calm environment; a relaxed meal will be more enjoyable and also will help digestion. Eating slowly, mindfully and chewing well will also give good health benefits for the mind and body.

Make gradual and careful changes to your diet that you can sustain. Unless you have a serious health condition, then I feel it is sensible, easier and more sustainable to make a slow integration of any new foods. Bring in the 'good' rather than cut out the 'bad', and try not to feel guilty if you stray from the 'healthy' options. Like a mindful meditation practise, just witness if you shift away and simply keep on bringing the awareness back; having patience with yourself is important.

Eat for you and follow your intuition. Use all the information out there, and then feel into what feels right for you. This may change from day to day and will definitely change with the seasons. What do you feel drawn to? Look at the seasons, your environment, daily activities, your cravings, emotions and what is going on for you. Step towards allowing your body to make decisions about food choices rather than the emotions or the mind.

EATING FOR BALANCE

I believe that finding balance is like weaving a web, it is intricate and takes work. We must shift and change each day, with how we are emotionally and physically, with each season, within our everyday lives, and our own bodies. When we study the elements and live in connection, we can use the energy of each element to balance our bodies at any time. Foods and flavours of the elements can be opening, expansive, strengthening, grounding, relaxing and/or nourishing. Choosing consciously can help to balance your own individual flow.

To understand how to eat more consciously, starting to study ourselves, in relation to the element system, is a beneficial place to start. We are all different. We all lead very unique lives with our own levels of activity and rest, and varying jobs and hobbies. Our personalities and patterns are also all very unique, this can be our constitution, ancestor patterns, or as a result from conditioning from our lives, especially childhood. It means we all have different balances of each of the elements within us. You may find you are particularly drawn to foods in one particular season and likewise can equally strongly dislike certain food categories. It's good to study the ones that have a big impact on you emotionally, as they could be key to understanding a part of yourself.

WORKING WITH THE FIVE ELEMENTS

Life and all parts within life form a beautiful cycle, I find the five elements are a great categorisation or mapping of this cycle and flow of life. Using this chart, you can hopefully begin building an understanding of the seasonal and element sections. For more detailed information on each element, see the introduction sections to each seasonal recipe section. You can then use this information to help you to identify some of your patterns, give you an overview of the cycle and your nature in relation to this. Then you can start to use the foods, flavours and cooking styles from each of the elements to bring in energies that fit for you at the right time, to nourish the body and different aspects of your personality and life. This can be seasonal, and within each day or week, which also helps to make our food really exciting and satisfying. The body and organs can be rebalanced and we can begin to heal any health problems.

Tree foods and cooking styles will support the liver and gallbladder, and help with creative ideas and clear decisions, also reducing unhealthy anger.

Water foods and cooking styles will support the kidneys and bladder, replenish the body, adding minerals and vitamins, giving more life energy, and reducing the emotion of fear.

Fire foods and cooking styles will support the heart and small intestines, help with zest and passion for life, activity and fun, reducing excessive inertia or cold heartedness.

Earth foods and cooking styles will support the stomach and spleen supporting love, nurture and nourishment.

Metal foods and cooking styles will support the lungs and large intestines, helping with letting go, order, structure, and healthy boundaries, and allow a healthy balance of the emotion of grief.

Healing with The Five Elements is a complex subject, and although this book may give you some general tips and ideas, I recommend seeing a macrobiotic counsellor if you want to delve into it deeper, and especially if you have a serious health condition that you may want support with.

balanced self: happy, friendly, active, sociable
imbalanced self: anxious, excessive laughter. nervousness

expansive active energy

color red

summer
•Fire

raw, lightly or quicly cooked

quinoa, bitter greens, lettuce, cucumber, courgettes, watercress red fruits, berries

organs: heart, small intestines

outwad growing foods

spring
•Tree

barley, leeks, celery, lemons fermented foods, pickles, sauerkraut, leafy greens

balanced self: planning, decision making, creative projects
imbalanced self: impatience, anger, frustration, inability to create action

colour green

sour taste

upward growing

organs: liver, gallbladder

opening, rising energy

pickled, pressed or light cooking, steaming

controls & extinguishes
controls & penetrates
controls & obstructs
controls & melts
controls & cuts
controls & damns

organs: stomach, spleen

Long cooking bringing out sweetness

grow on the earth

late summer
•Earth

colour brown or orange

balanced self: self love, imagination, sympathy, able to receive love, empathy
imbalanced self: worry, moaning, putting other first or unable to support self or others

millet, sweet rice. onions, swede, white cabbage, squash, pumpkin

sweet taste

winter
•Water
color purple or black

inward & restful energy

balanced self: willpower, vitality, healthy sexuality
imbalanced self: fearful, selfdoubt,

buckwheat, fish, sea vegetables sea salt, miso, shoyu, burdock

organs: kidneys, bladder

food from the sea

autumn
•Metal

rooting, completion energy   pungent taste
Pressure cooked, dry cooking, longest cooking, baking   downward growing

Medium or short grain brown rice, root veg eg. carrots, mooli, radish. garlic, ginger
balanced self: organised, ordered, able to complete to let go, allow change
imbalanced self: grief, melancholy, scattered, obsessivly tidy
organs: lungs, large intestines

creates and supports

creates and supports

creates and supports

creates and supports

This section is to satisfy the mind, it's based on western nutritional research and shows that it is definitely possible to get the right balance of nutrition for our bodies from a plant-based diet. From this research, we can see that dark green leafy vegetables are one of the most vital foods, my favourite saying is Kale is King.

WHAT OUR BODIES NEED NUTRITIONALLY &
WHERE TO FIND THIS IN A WHOLE FOOD DIET

Protein gives us the amino acids needed to maintain proper health, helping build muscles, repair tissue and maintaining an effective immune and hormonal system. Make sure to include a mix of grains, pulses, seeds and vegetables each day, especially if you don't eat fish.

Fish	Seeds (pumpkin,
Shellfish	sesame, sunflower)
Beans & Lentils	Whole Grains
Nuts (Almonds, Hazelnuts)	(oats, rye)

Fat provides energy; the body needs some stored fat to prevent heat loss and transport the sex hormones. Essential fats that our body needs can be obtained with unsaturated fat from vegetable sources. Although fat is essential, it needs limiting to avoid becoming over weight.

Olive oil &	Nuts and
other vegetable oils	nut butters
Seeds	
(sesame and sunflower)	

Fibre is needed to help absorption of nutrients, and to stimulate waste excretion and substances that combat against free radical damage. It is very easy to consume plenty of fibre when eating a whole food diet.

Wholegrains	Fruit and vegetables
Pulses	

26

Vitamin A is needed for growth, healthy skin, good vision and tooth enamel.

Oily fish (salmon, mackerel)	vegetables (spinach
Carrots	broccoli)
Dark green leafy	

The B vitamins, B1, B2, B3, folic acid, B5, B6 and B12.
These are essential for growth and development of healthy nervous system. They also digest food and help convert it into energy.

Dark green leafy	Fish and shellfish
vegetables	Eggs
Nuts (walnuts. brazils)	Vitamin E
Beans	

Vitamin K helps the blood to clot and maintains strong bones. It is produced in the bacteria in a healthy gut so a general whole food diet will ensure adequate Vitamin K.

Dark green leafy	(broccoli and kale)
vegetables	Carrots

Magnesium is used in the body to build strong bones, release energy from muscles, regulate body temperature, and help the body absorb and metabolise various other vitamins and minerals.

Whole grains	vegetables
Dark green leafy	Bananas and apricots

Vitamin D is an important vitamin that works with calcium for essential bone formation.

Sardines	Salmon
Mackerel	Sunlight

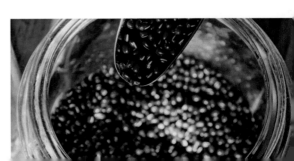

Sodium needs to be balanced in the body. Eating too much will lead to low levels of potassium and perhaps cravings for liquids and deserts as your body tries to regain balance. However, it is also important to not have too little in your diet.

Sea vegetables	Sauerkraut
Quality salt	Olives
Miso and shoyu	

Potassium works in conjunction with sodium to regulate the body's water balance, heart rhythm, nerve impulses and muscle function. It is important to get a good balance as sodium and potassium work like a see saw; when the sodium level increases, the potassium level decreases and vice versa.

Fish and shellfish	Potatoes and other
Whole grains	fresh vegetables
Nuts and seeds	Fruits and fruit juices

Calcium is needed for strong bones and teeth. There are many great sources without the need for excessive dairy foods

Dark leafy greens,	Nuts
e.g. kale and watercress	esp. Almonds,
Sesame seeds	Hazelnuts
Soya beans	Sea Vegetables
Tempeh, tofu	eg. dulse and wakame

Vitamin D works with calcium for essential bone formation.

Sardines	Salmon
Mackerel	Sunlight

28

Iron is needed for healthy blood and mussels. Make sure you include good amounts of food with iron in your daily diet

Oily fish,	Pumpkin seeds
squid, mussels	Sesame seeds
whole grains	Dark leafy greens
Soya,	e.g. parsley, watercress
Chickpeas,	kale, broccoli
lentils,	Sea Vegetables
kidney beans	eg. dulse and wakame

Vitamin C is needed for growth, healthy body tissue and healing wounds. It also helps the body absorb iron.

Dark leafy greens (e.g.	Cauliflower
kale and watercress)	Strawberries,
Broccoli	blackcurrants,
Cabbage	citrus fruit

A balance of **acid and alkaline.** Look to balance your acid and alkaline; overall acidity can lead to poor health. It puts a strain on your body which fights to combat the imbalance, including using calcium to remove acid through the urine. A common western diet is full of acidic foods, meat, dairy, sugar. In a whole food diet, grains and dried beans are moderately acidic and vegetables are alkaline. To achieve a good balance, choose mainly from the low acid and alkaline foods, and make sure vegetables are a good proportion of your diet.

High Alkaline:
Sea salt, Miso and
Shoy, Sauerkraut

Low alkaline:
Sea vegetables
Green vegetables
Root vegetables

High acid:
Fruit, Sugar, Vinegar,
Alcohol, Meat, White
flour products

Low acid:
Grains, Wholemeal
breads, Dried beans,
Fish, Eggs, Nuts

CONSCIOUS COOKING

MINDFUL SHOPPING AND COOKING

Great cooking starts with great ingredients. Use the best quality ingredients you can, organic and minimally handled or processed. Organic food has far more taste and is better for the body, as you will not be consuming unnecessary pesticides used to protect non organic food. Choose locally grown foods, sign up for a delivered organic vegetable box, use local farmer's markets and forage for wild foods. We take on the energy of the foods we eat, so work on avoiding any foods with a negative energy, particularly non organic meats and dairy. If we buy and eat animal products from a source of unhappy animals, we are taking that energy into our bodies.

Use good quality pans and utensils. Stainless steel is my preferable material for cooking, as it does not leak anything into the food during the cooking process. I also love iron woks and use these for many things, including frying, curries and larger one pot meals. For utensils, I use stainless steel and my favourite of all the wooden spoon. I avoid aluminium and plastics, choosing to store food in ceramic bowls covered with a small plate.

The energy you hold when cooking is going to impact the food. Make sure you cook in a calm environment and cook in the right space and frame of mind. If you cook with love and good intent, you will create beautifully balanced and energising food; if you cook when you are angry, you will inevitably not enjoy the final eating experience.

Recipes are always interesting and good to follow, allowing inspiration, however, you will inevitably be putting your own energy into the dish. It is interesting when you see the same dish cooked by different people, it will always be unique to each individual; I have come to the conclusion that one of the most important ingredients that is in every single dish is the cook's energy!

On a practical note with recipes, be aware that food types and oven/hob types and many other small variations, eg. oven temperature, flame size, vegetable size, will impact the cooking and the recipe's final result . I recommend you cook with your intuition rather than rigidly following any recipe. This will also allow you to learn to adapt recipes to suit what you have in the vegetable box and cupboard and begin creating your own recipes.

VARIETY

There is such a vast array of wonderful foods once you step away from habit patterns of meat and dairy. There are so many vegetables, grains, vegetarian sources of proteins and great seasonings that will give your food variety and excitement. Once I learnt to cook with all these new ingredients in a successful way, I didn't look back; my diet and is rich and satisfying.

Using variety is also key in a plant-based diet so that we receive all the nutrients that we need in the body. See chapter 'What Our Bodies Need'. Meat provides many vitamins and minerals. It is possible to find all these from plants, and including a variety will ensure a good and eclectic balance. If you choose to become vegan, it is even more essential that you include a good mix of foods so the body is being properly nourished.

As well as a variety of different foods, use tasty seasonings and a mix of cooking styles for your meals: baking, steaming, fermenting, sauteing, deep frying, stews, soups, salads, deserts. Making food tasty and nourishing satisfies our earth energy, helping keep the balance. Lots of people remark how tasty my food is, it's key to sustaining this way of eating. This is where the five elements really become useful as we can use them, and the variety of flavours and cooking styles to enhance our meals and create a satisfying eating experience that we are more likely to sustain.

CONSCIOUS CHOPPING

Being mindful as you chop your vegetables will enliven your meals. A simple choice of how to cut ingredients for a dish will add interest and also a great energy to your meal. Be aware of the energy lines/ meridians of the vegetable and cut with this awareness. Cutting diagonally is one of my favourite ways, this gives good balance to the vegetable.

When linking ingredients within a dish, chop and choose similar sizes to link grains, beans and vegetables and produce an energetically balanced meal. You can align the energy of the foods you cook with by the chopping methods you choose.

On a practical note, making sure you chop each individual type of vegetable the same size will mean they cook equally i.e, pumpkin to be baked or onions to be sauted.

Some of my favourite cutting tips:

Use a variety of cutting styles: large or small chunks, diced, half moons, batons, diagonal slices, diagonal half moons, rings.

For onions, first, I always half down middle with the meridians, this makes them easy to then peel, From here, you can choose the shape you want.

For squash and pumpkin, it's good to start by cutting down the middle length ways and scoop out the seeds. If the skin is soft, you don't always need to peel. Dice or cut into chunks to cook.

For carrots, I always tend to start diagonally, then from here, you can baton or dice. See picture.

Being mindful seasonally, it's great to cut thicker in winter for longer cooking warming stews, and smaller dicing or grating in summer for quick cooked lighter foods, stir frys and salads.

Who are you and what would you like within your life? Choosing foods to support you and your lifestyle can be key to flourishing in your life and into who you want to be. A plant-based diet can be suitable for anyone but it's important to eat for you, we are all different. When I came to this way of eating, I was significantly detached from my feminine energy; it's been an amazing journey to uncover it again, to choose foods that suit this energy and embrace how I want to feel. However, this is not gender specific, these are arcetypal energies, and we all have both masculine and feminine energies within us. You can find the balance you prefer for yourself by eating the foods that welcome and enhance this. Look at your activity levels, your job, your choice of how you spend your spare time. Do you work outside in a physically demanding way or at a desk? Do you prefer yoga and meditation or running, swimming or the gym? We can eat foods that suit us and our life style or if you feel you want to make changes then you can choose options that invite more of that energy in; but remember you may need to change your lifestyle too if you really want to make a significant difference.

COOKING FOR WHO WE ARE & WHO WE WANT TO BE

Supporting feminine energy

Feminine energy is soft and light, opening and gentle. There may be less physical strength in the body and muscles. If you prefer a gentler way of being, then these foods will suit you. For a woman, one possible reason you may want to follow this way is if menstruation has become painful, heavy or contracting. Or perhaps going into a perimenopausal phase, you may choose this energy to allow a gentle flow. To support feminine energy and promote softness, avoid dry baked foods, meat and eggs, and excessively salty foods. Prepare softer, gentle foods with more moisture and sweetness. Include more vegetables and beans in your daily diet; even within the plant-based diet, you can balance more for feminine energy in this way. Include lots of foods from the earth section, soups and stews, less grains, and healthy deserts, as ways to promote opening sweetness.

Recipe Suggestions

millet risotto	page 115	aduki squash soup	page 176
nishime	page 127	chickpea squash curry	page 116
apple dessert	page 159	wild green vegetables	page 23
pumpkin soup	page 123	meadow sweet dessert	page 128
gram pancakes	page 117	beetroot soup	Page 112
blackbean soup	page 183		

Supporting masculine energy

Masculine energy is a stronger, more dynamic energy, with action and getting things done. There may be more muscle strength and endurance. It is important to make sure you are getting good levels of protein, it may even be that more animal foods are needed, such as fish or even some meat; however, remember that many plant-based foods have protein, especially Seitan that has more protein per gram than beef; so if you are a vegan, it is also possible to make it work if you are careful and include a wide variety. For extra energy, especially if working outside in colder weather, then you can include stronger heartier foods, use the metal foods in particular, include whole grains, pressure cooked, some fried and baked foods.

Recipe Suggestions

Foods for families/ children

Family foods need to be fun and exciting. And also in my experience, children like simple foods, but also familiar ones, so you may have to gently introduce any new foods. Children thrive off the sweet taste, as this is expansive for them as they grow. So using good quality sweetness and plenty of fruit and vegetables will support this. I also like to make sure they are also getting enough vitamins and minerals with perhaps a little fish or even the odd egg. If a child is vegan, it's important to get a healthy balance of foods so that they are getting all they need. I always include a spoonful of gomasio in my children's porridge for calcium and broccoli every day too.

Foods for nourishing the body

Sometimes, for varying reasons, we can loose more weight than is ideal for us. This can become as equal an issue as excessive weight gain. It can happen from declined eating, maybe from an eating disorder or sometimes when people turn away from meat and dairy, the body begins to adapt to plant-based foods. As well as weight loss you can feel into if you have become undernourished, as it may effect energy levels and possibly the condition of your skin. If you are completely vegan, you may need to be careful; make sure you are getting variety in your diet with plenty of grains, pulses and vegetables. Also make sure you are not consuming sugar instead of vital calories from protein and carbohydrate sources.

To boost the body, gain weight and increase nourishment you can, eat a richer diet with hearty grain dishes, fats, vegetables and plant-based proteins.

Foods for cleansing the body

Cleansing the body can be a great thing, to not support weight loss, but also anybody can benefit from detoxing even if weight loss is not an issue. A cleanse will enliven the body and increase energy by clearing out impurities.

As you cleanse the body, this will be able to release toxins making for better digestive and overall health. This may be suitable if you feel your body is sluggish from having eaten a diet heavy in animal foods or processed foods. Recommended is eating fresh vegetables and fruits, light and opening foods, and drinking cleansing teas. All the foods from the spring/tree element section are ideal.

Recipe Suggestions for cleansing the body

nettle soup	page 52	nettle lemon tea	page 77
beetroot & cabbage		miso & ginger soup	page 151
salad	page 127	rosehip tea	page 164
barley risotto	page 54	wild green salad	page 64
steamed turnips	page 155	lemon mousse	page 74

Supporting spiritual development

The food we eat impacts our life experience; if your aim is to raise your vibration and allow spiritual development, then eating consciously is crucial. I began my holistic awareness through teaching yoga but it was only when I found the macrobiotic diet and cleaned up my diet that it stepped up a level. Eating for spiritual enlightenment is about eating pure foods; these would be non-animal, unprocessed, organic. Most of the foods in this book have this clean energy; however if you do want to accelerate your spiritual growth, I would definitely recommend a vegan diet, as this is guaranteed to be most pure. Whole grains, pulses, vegetables, and sea vegetables are all perfect. Eating to connect to spirit and increase awareness to earth can be supported by foraging for wild foods, mindful eating and chewing your foods well.

Recipe Suggestions for supporting spiritual development

steamed kale & leek	page 185	winter vegetable salad	page 185
rosehip kanten	page 157	aduki squash soup	page 176
sweet sour veg	page 59	leafy salad from wild	page 64
wild pesto	page 53	wholegrain porridge	page 188
broccoli & pea soup	page 83	sweetcorn chowder	page 113

This section is an introduction to some of the foods used in this book and successful ways to cook and introduce then into your diet. There is so much variety, and an eclectic mix of flavours and energies. These ingredients are great, as they can be stored in the cupboard and in lovely glass jars, and can easily form the essence of a meal. If I'm not sure what to cook, I stand looking at my bean and grain jars for inspiration, something exciting always takes shape.

INGREDIENTS IN THE STORE CUPBOARD AND COOKING TIPS

GRAINS

All grains are best cooked with the exact part water to grain, allowing the final grain to be fully cooked and tasty once the water has been absorbed. Some grains like to be soaked prior to cooking, and some like to be toasted which brings out their nutty flavour. To toast, use a medium flame and move the grains regularly so they don't burn; they will smell nutty once they are ready. For soaking, cover with water and leave for a few hours or overnight if possible. Whether toasting or soaking, once you add the water, bring to the boil and then turn down to very low; I recommend using a flame spreader, as these prevent burning. Cook with tight lid, or in a pressure cooker, until the water is absorbed and the grain is soft. Once you get this right, it's very satisfying and the grains are super tasty. It's good to add a pinch of salt or a stick of kombu whilst cooking, as this adds flavour and alkaline to the acidic grain.

Quinoa

This grain is actually a seed, although it acts like a grain, and it is a great source of plant protein. Enjoy quinoa as a side grain dish like rice, as a base for a salad, or as a breakfast porridge.
To cook:
1 part quinoa to 2 part water. 25 minutes. Toasting recommended.

Millet

This is a really flexible grain; it's sweet and nutritious and slightly alkaline; millet makes a great alternative to mash and can be also used in soups, stews, risotto style dishes, burgers and porridge.
To cook:
1 part millet to 2.5 or 3 part water. 30 minutes. Toasting recommended.

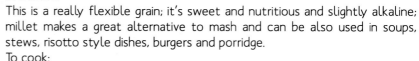

Buckwheat

Buckwheat is a strong grain with an intense energy, good for occasional use and great in winter. Use in burgers, bread or as a side dish, its flour makes great gluten free pancakes and batter.

To cook:

1 part buckwheat to 2 part water. 20 minutes. Toasting recommended.

Barley

Barley is a delicate and cleansing grain that cools and relaxes the body. It is flexible and works well on its own or in a soup or stew; I also sometimes use it with short grain brown to add lightness to the dish.

To cook:

1 part barley to 2 part water. 45 minutes. Soaking recommended.

Oats

Creamy, delicious and satisfying, oats are a winner every time. I use whole oat groats in our porridge but also enjoy the rolled oats in flapjacks and deserts.

To cook:

1 part oat groat to 2 part water. Or in porridge, 1 part oat groat to 5 parts water. 50 minutes. Soaking recommended.

Corn

Fresh corn is delicious and nutritious. This is a great grain for children, as it's lovely and sweet. Corn flours and polenta are also tasty and fun to use.

To cook polenta:

1 part polenta to 3 part water. 20 minutes. Pack into a tin and cool. For polenta porridge, use 1 part polenta to 4 water.

Rice

There are so many different types, choose from long grain, basamati, wild rice, medium grain and short grain. I always choose the wholegrain, brown.

To cook:

1 part rice to 2 part water. 50 minutes. Soaking recommended.

PULSES

This section includes lentils, beans and peas. Most lentils are cooked with 3 part water to one part lentils. Smaller beans such as aduki and black beans are the same as lentils. With the bigger beans, I tend to use larger amounts of water and strain once they are cooked. All beans benefit from soaking; however with small beans, you can cook without soaking, simply increase the cooking time. Once you have soaked your larger beans, 8-12 hours, it's preferable to change the soaking water. There is much debate over black and aduki beans as to whether what you loose in goodness out weighs the toxins that remain if you don't refresh the water. I was always taught it was good to use the soaking water, and intuitively, it looks and feels so rich and dense in nutrients I prefer this way. However, the choice is yours. All beans benefit from adding kombu to the cooking water as this improves the digestibility of them and also adds alkaline.

Chickpeas

A versatile tight, round and creamy pulse that is packed, full of protein, making it nourishing for the earth element. The chickpea is great for hummus, falafels, soups, stews and curries.
To cook:
Soaking recommenced. Refresh the water after soaking and cover with plenty of fresh water, cook 1-1 1/2 hours.

Black beans

High in protein and fibre and full of goodness, black beans are great. They are sweet and earthy and nourishing for the nervous system and feminine energy.
To cook:
1 part bean to 3 parts water. Soaking recommended.

Kidney beans

A great bean full of goodness, dark red and shaped like a kidney; however, they also come in white called cannalini beans. They are a great bean for fire energy.
To cook:
Soaking recommenced. Refresh the water after soaking and cover with plenty of fresh water, cook 1-1 1/2 hours.

Aduki beans

An amazing small red bean used commonly in macrobiotic and ayurverdic diets for savoury and sweet dishes. They are very balancing and nourishing for the kidneys and bladder. Great in soups and stews, combined with squash, and for red dragon pie.

To cook:

1 part bean to 3 parts water. Soaking recommended, cooking time = 1 hour.

Lentils

Lentils are fantastic. They come in many colours and sizes. Red, green, puy, brown. They are all tasty and really flexible; make dahl, and use them in stews and soups. They are perfect for quick and nutritious meals.

To cook:

1 part lentil to 3 parts water. Soaking optional.

Split peas

Dried shelled and split 'peas'. Yellow and green split peas are nutritious and tasty, used in split pea soup, dahl and stews.

To cook:

1 part pea to 3 parts water. Soaking optional.

Butter beans

Butter bean are a well-rounded source of nutrition, like all pulses, rich in protein, fibre, iron and B vitamins. They are soft and creamy. I like to puree them like a hummus, or put them in soups and stews.

To cook:

Soaking recommenced. Refresh the water after soaking and cover with plenty of fresh water, cook 1-1 1/2 hours.

Soya beans

Great versatile beans that are used for many things. I am wary of overly processed soya products, but find the inclusion of fresh and dried soya beans, tempeh and good quality tofu really valuable for our family diet.

To cook:

Soaking recommenced. Refresh the water after soaking and cover with plenty of fresh water, cook 1-1 1/2 hours.

SEA VEGETABLES

Sea vegetables are a super food with the deep primal energy of the sea. They are a great way of getting vitamins and minerals in the diet, especially calcium and iron; however, it's important to use them in moderation, as too much can lead to excessive iodine levels in the body. They also add flavour without the need for excessive salt, and as they have a gentler energy than salt, this is great for our bodies. You can buy them dried but also forage for yourself, a lot of seaweeds you find will be edible.

Agar
This is an interesting sea vegetable that acts like gelatin. When you add agar flakes to boiling water, it dissolves and once it is completely cool, it sets. Use agar flakes to make aspic, or kanten, a jelly dish. Use 1 tbsp per cup of liquid for best results.

Wakame
This is a great in soups, salads and stews; it's particularly great in miso soup.
Add into a stew whilst cooking or soak and chop adding raw to salads into a miso type soup towards the end of cooking.

Arame and Hijiki
Arame is a mild, sweet and easy to prepare sea vegetable that grows in deep waters. Hiziki is a similar but thicker brown algae that grows on the ocean floor. Both are high in calcium, nutritious and tasty.
To cook: Soak in water for 10 minutes until soft and cook for 20-30 minutes.

Kelp/kombu
kelp is a great local sea vegetable that is an abundant source of vitamins and minerals such as iodine, potassium, magnesium, calcium, iron.
To cook:
Long cooking needed so use in soups or stews and when cooking beans, where it will disperse into the dish adding goodness, or use to add flavour to stock, grains, and vegetables, and remove before eating, with an option to reuse it again for another dish.

Dulse

Dulse is commonly found on the Irish coast. It is easy to prepare; soak until soft and add raw to salads, or place in soups and stews. This is a really tasty, flexible and local sea vegetable. A good one to start with if you are new to them.

Nori

Nori is the Japanese word for dried edible seaweed sheets made from a species of red algae called Porphyra. Sushi is the most common use for these dried sheets. You can buy them toasted and so totally prepared and ready for making sushi. You can also buy nori not toasted which is a little trickier to prepare, check the pack before buying, so you know which sort you are purchasing.

SEASONINGS

There is a selection of great seasonings that can add interest to a meal. They are all tasty addition to stirfrys, vegetable dishes, soups, stew and/ or dressings.

Ume plum seasoning is one of my favourites. Ume's are fruits, from Japan, referred to as plums but are actually more closely related to apricots. You can buy them pickled and whole, or as ume puree, and with shiso, as this vinegar like seasoning, which gives a salty, sour, sweet flavour. Delicious.

Shoyu is a fantastic seasoning, originating from ancient China and made by fermenting soya beans with roasted wheat. As well as having a unique and pleasurable flavour, it has nutritional and medicinal properties, rich in minerals, antioxidants and aids the digestion of beans and grains. For a similar product that is wheat free, use tamari.

Mirin is a sweet rice vinegar that is tasty and an essential condiment used in Japanese cuisine. It is a type of rice wine similar to sake, but with a lower alcohol content and higher sugar content. The sugars form naturally during the fermentation process which means no extra sugars are needed. The best quality I have found is Mirwaki Mirin from Clearspring.

Rice vinegar or apple cider vinegar are both quality vinegars that make a great impact. Vinegar has also been around since ancient times since it was discovered that wild acetic-acid bacteria could turn alcohol into a great tasting preservative. All vinegars have a great zingy taste that stimulates the appetite and awakens the taste buds. Rice vinegar and apple cider vinegar with mother are good quality vinegars that are enjoyable and effective as seasonings or preservatives.

Mustard is a pungent, strong flavoured condiment made from mustard seeds. Use to enhance or complement meals, nice as a balance to heavier meals with animal proteins. Choose from djon, English or wholegrain, or use the whole seed like a spice.

Tahini is a bitter spread made from ground sesame seeds. So it's full of goodness and calcium. It is also called sesame paste or sesame butter as its like peanut butter but made from sesame seeds. Tahini made from unhulled sesame seeds is darker and more nutritious than tahini made from hulled seeds, it is also more bitter, but I always prefer the least processed option. It's great in dressings and I use it often in tofu to create a richness and add nutrition.

Nut butters are a great addition to many meals, deserts and good in porridge; a tasty delight in vegan cooking. A nut butter is made by grinding nuts into a paste. The result has a high fat content paste that can be spread like dairy butter. Nut butters that I often use are almond butter, cashew butter, hazelnut butter or peanut butter.

Miso is a fabulous fermented healing food that is rich in vitamins, minerals, an antioxidant, and is also alkaline. It is a traditional Japanese seasoning produced by fermenting soybeans with salt and koji and sometimes rice, barley or other ingredients. High in protein and rich in vitamins and minerals, miso plays an important nutritional role in whole food diets. You can buy many different sorts, my favaourites are barley miso and sweet miso. Use to flavour soups and stews, and a great addition to a dressing.

I use a few different types of alternative sweeteners. Even though these are far less processed than sugar, remember they are still sweet and further from balanced on the scale, so it's good to use them wisely. However, these alternatives can really support coming away from sugary products and helping to beat addictions, whilst still creating a balanced energy of sweetness. Once stepping away and finding alternatives to white sugar, there is no going back. Cakes and overly sweet products now make my pulse race, and I feel an unhealthy stimulation in the body. All the sweeteners listed below have less of an impact on the body keeping equilibrium and reducing cravings and blood sugar imbalance. Bringing up 3 children, it's great to have these sweeteners so I can make sure they are not being negatively impacted by excessive sugary products, yet they are still enjoying the sweetness of life.

SWEETNESS

Apple concentrate is made by pressing and reducing apples. I find it a really handy sugar substitute for many things as it's natural and not overly processed. However, I recommend choosing good quality and organic which will have ensured that some of the apples' nutritional value will have been retained; I like Suma's. Often the flavour of the apple can come through when you are using it as a sweeter, but I find this enjoyable. In my kitchen, I use it regularly for dressings, some deserts, wild fruit jams and fruit syrups.

Rice syrup is a fantastic sugar substitute, and one of our oldest sweeteners, coming from ancient oriental times where I have read that it was only processed in sacred places! Rice malt syrup is the best quality you can buy and the lowest on the GI index, as there is significant levels of maltose that takes far longer to digest than glucose. As the process to turn the rice into rice syrup is simple, rice syrup also retains many of rice's nutrients. This is one of my favourite sweeteners, as it is healthy, versatile and tasty.

Barley malt syrup is a thick and malty sweetener that is deep in colour and rich in flavour. Like rice malt syrup, the process to make the syrup is simple and unobtrusive to the whole grain so the final product feels sacred and nutritious. I use barley malt in ginger bread, puddings, hot chocolate and some of my bread recipes. Its great flavour can really add interest to a desert. When buying barley malt syrup, choose the most pure products; I use Clearspring.

Dried Fruits are highly nutritious, a great way to enjoy sweetness and to sweeten deserts. They are natural and close to the original state of the fruit, in fact the nutritional content is not reduced very much by the drying process. They are medium to low on glycemic index, which is another bonus. In my kitchen, I commonly use sultanas, raisins dates, prunes, figs and apricots. Dates make a great syrup for cakes, sultanas and raisins sweeten porridge; apricots make a great mousee or sweeten savoury dishes; they can all make tasty cakes and puddings. What a great addition to a wholefood kitchen.

Amazake is a sweet product that comes totally from grain, made by fermenting rice or millet with a cultured rice called koji. As the grain is fermented, it becomes amazingly sweet and creamy resulting in this delicious sweetener. It's a great thing to use as a dairy substitute for satisfyingly creamy deserts or puddings. I also enjoy it with oat milk or water and cocoa powder as a hot chocolate.

Maple syrup is a gift from the Gods, it feels so special and sacred. It comes from the sap, made by sugar maple trees that rises up and is harvested in the early spring. Therefore, it strongly embodies the tree energy, so use mindfully as it's very sweet and opening. Also make sure the maple syrup you buy is 'pure' with nothing added, choose a high grade that is minimally tampered with. However, it is pretty expensive; in our house, I use it for occasional cakes and deserts, especially for birthdays.

Vanilla is a sweetener and flavouring from orchids of the genus vanilla, primarily from the Mexican species, flat-leaved vanilla. You can buy the whole pod or an extract, it's not cheap but buying the best quaity possible is ideal, with no added sugar. Luckily, you only need a small amount to add a sweet and beautiful flavour to cakes and deserts.

THE RIGHT KIND OF FATS

There are a lot of theories out in the world about fats; due to the weight issues in our culture, fat has caused a great stir. Are we eating too much, which kinds are good and which are bad, should we heat them or not? I sit in a camp which likes fats; fats are not the baddies, in fact, our bodies need essential fats to function properly. However, like sweetness, we need the right kind of fats, in a good balance, for the body to flourish.

There are many different types of fats and not all of them are good for the body. Saturated fats, found in meat, can increase cholesterol and LDL (unhealthy cholesterol) in the body which leads to health risks, especially for the heart. A lot of fat in a western diet comes from dairy, but as well as the fact these are saturated fats; in my opinion, dairy is a product for a baby animal, not for us as humans. Since giving up dairy, I feel healthier and more empowered, not relying on a cow's milk to give me sustenance. My most grievance with dairy is the industry itself; if you do choose to include dairy in your diet, make sure it is the best quality, organic and from animals that are well cared for. We take on the energy of our food, so I wonder what are we consuming when we eat dairy from a non-organic source?

In the bad camp is also the 'trans fats'; these are especially found in processed foods. Any foods with hydrogenated oils or fats in them are most likely to contain trans fats. These processed fatty foods, fried foods, takeaway food, biscuits, cakes and pastries, energetically jar with the body, as they have come so far away from what Mother Earth naturally provides for us.

Energetically and nutritionally, fats from a healthy source are best, and the research from Western nutritionists back this up. The guidelines point towards unsaturated fats; the two main types are mono-unsaturated and polyunsaturated. Mono-unsaturated fats raise HDL (good cholesterol) and lower LDL; good sources are olives and olive oil, peanuts and peanut oil, seeds, avocados, almonds, cashews, hazelnuts, and spreads made from these nuts. Polyunsaturated fats help to maintain healthy cholesterol levels and provide essential fatty acids; good sources are flaxseed, pine nuts, sesame seeds, sunflower seeds, and walnuts. Key fats to eat are the essential fats with omega 3 and 6, which cannot be produced by your body. Omega 3s are the king and sources include flax seeds, pumpkin seeds, soybean and its products such as tofu and tempeh, walnuts, and dark green vegetables.

I find to eat a balanced and varied wholefood diet will ensure plentiful amounts of the essential fats our bodies need whilst also nourishing us on an energetic level.

SPRING

AND THE ELEMENT OF TREE

Spring is the start of the new cycle, life begins to burst into action. I love the gentle but profound opening where life emerges once again out of the stillness of winter. We see the first signs of spring appear pretty early, with the snowdrops, crocus and then primroses. The rising energy feels like it starts around Imbolc (beginning of February). It's really nice to mark this space and know that the warmer weather and light is on its way. By early March, I can feel the energy of spring coming stronger and stronger, especially when we get a sunny day or two, and when daffodils begin to pop up. Shoots and buds appear on plants and trees; animals and birds begin to prepare for their their babies; fertility, birth and new life surrounds us. The sun feels warmer, freshness is in the air, and spring is coming. Spring Equinox, on or around the 21st March, marks the official arrival of spring and is another great point to mark in the cycle of the year. Here at Sunny Brow, we celebrate with ritual and ceremony to honour the air element, the balance of masculine feminine, birth and fertility. It's a good time to release anything unwanted from the old cycle and bring in awareness of new goals and ambitions.

It feels great to spring clean; the house, garden and our bodies all benefit from a clear out. It's a perfect time to cleanse and to form commitments for new growth of mind, body and soul. Nature provides cleansing and opening foods to open and detox the body. After the more contractive energy of winter, these foods are a great way to support the natural flow in this season. There is much fun in bringing in the new shoots of spring into the kitchen to cleanse and freshen the body. All the sour flavours of the new leaves are perfect for this job. Green is the colour of the season, leaves and greenery are bursting open everywhere.

In season in the spring garden: purple sprouting broccoli, cabbage, spring greens, leeks, lettuce, rocket, radishes, rhubarb, salad onions, asparagus, cauliflowers, celeriac, lettuce In season in the wild: sorrel, nettles, dandelion, watercress,

wintercress, burdock stems, plantain, wild garlic, jack-by-the-hedge, lady's mantle, hawthorn and beech leaves, pine shoots

This time of year corresponds to the Tree or Wood element. To understand this element, we need to study and understand the trees. Stand next to a tree and make a connection. Feel the strong centred energy, the growth, the connection to heaven and earth, their flexibility and strong sustaining roots. A tree is a great representation of life, its cycle marks out and is very aligned with the seasons; its connection to the earth and movement to the heavens shows this is a very spiritual element. It is about creation, growth and new life. It is about budding shoots, creative ideas and the beginning of putting ideas into action with planning and decisions. Tree or Wood, energy is the beginning of the flow of life force, birth, growth and development. This energy is about transformation, taking essence and turning it into manifestation. The organs related to tree are liver and gallbladder. The energetic role of our liver is military leader and the gallbladder is his second in command. When it is in good balance, we are able to put creativity into action; an idea from birth until it's in full action is led by Tree. We are in harmony and can flow with ease. In good balance, we have nourishment from roots, growth and flexibility to adapt to life and the flow of change.

However, Tree energy can easily build up within the body if there is not enough movement and release. Tree relies on movement, growth and flow, for harmony, if we go out of balance, Tree energy can easily can get 'stuck'. If the Tree stops flowing, the energy builds up and we can become prisoner in the body, emotions become held inside; physical symptoms can be arthritis, cramps, PMS, headaches, migraines, anger and irritability. Muscles and sinews can get hard and tighten, causing our body to become overly contracted and rigid. Liver lines can form in the brow, we can become stubborn, overly frustrated and only able to relate to our own decisions. Those with too much Tree will have a tendency to over work but can also become lacking in vision and cannot see the 'wood from the trees'.

If there is too much Tree energy, then we can do many things to balance this out; eat all green leaves and plants, get out in the wild, forage, connect to the earth and what grows. Cleanse the liver with juices and infusions, eat sour foods, add dressings to a meal with sour flavours, eat lemons, fermented foods and drink lemon teas, and also good can be the Fire element foods too. Wood is controlled by Metal, so make sure you don't eat too many baked products, especially baked white flour, bread and crackers. Reduce foods that are dry and include softer opening foods that are cooked quickly, eat pressed salads and leafy greens. Reduce excessive contracting things including meats, eggs, overwork and stress. Reduce fat, and processed foods, and anything that puts a demand on the body and organs. Invite into your life more gentle, creative projects, dancing and moving the body in a flowing way, meditations with a tree, and deep breathing, especially the outside in nature and the spring air.

Problems when the Tree energy is lacking are less common. But what happens if we become uprooted when we are no longer able to receive nourishment to blossom. Symptoms can be depression, low self-esteem, inability to make decisions or ideas, or only able to think creatively but not be able to put things into planning and action. Eating and cooking with Tree foods and cooking styles is good in moderation, as is connecting to plants and Mother Earth, but primarily look to include Earth and Water foods, in the late summer and winter sections to support and nourish.

Food and cooking styles to support the Tree element and in spring:
Barley, oats, wheat & rye; leeks, celery, any green vegetables, green peppers, string beans, broccoli (esp. purple sprouting), larger green lentils and green slit peas; tart fruits: lemons, rhubarb, green sour apples; fermented foods, sauerkraut, kimchee, pickles, tempeh and tofu, spring leaves, sprouted beans & lentils; quick cooking, stewing & steaming, pressed salads.

High in vitamins and minerals, especially calcium, and great for cleansing the body, nettles are great addition to any soup or stew. This dish uses nettles as the star ingredient, it's a satisfying wild food recipe that's very simple, nettles love our wild garden so we never have a shortage of ingredients!

NETTLE AND WILD GARLIC SOUP

Serves 4-6
4 cup freshly picked nettles
1 cup wild garlic leaves
1 large carrot, chopped
1/2 medium celeriac or swede
1 large onion, chopped
1 large potato, chopped
1 tbsp oil
Seasonings: ume vinegar, apple concentrate

Saute the onions, carrots and celeriac in the oil with a pinch of salt for about 5 minutes. Add 5 cups of water and the potatoes and bring to the boil. Simmer until vegetables are soft, about 10-15 minutes. Add nettles and wild garlic and cook for a further two minutes. Season to taste with the ume vinegar and apple concentrate.

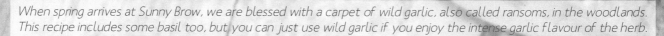

When spring arrives at Sunny Brow, we are blessed with a carpet of wild garlic, also called ransoms, in the woodlands. This recipe includes some basil too, but you can just use wild garlic if you enjoy the intense garlic flavour of the herb.

WILD GARLIC PESTO

Makes about 1 cup of pesto:
1 1/2 cups basil leaves
1 1/2 cups wild garlic leaves
1/2 cup sunflower or pumpkin seeds, toasted
1/2 cup olive oil
1 tbsp lemon juice
1 tbsp white miso, ume paste or a tsp salt

Blend all the ingredients together. Add more seasonings to taste if you wish. Serve as a dip, spread or great with pasta

Barley is a light and opening grain, which makes it great for spring or if a less heavy grain dish appeals. Adding new season nettles, leeks and wild garlic gives this risotto a wild twist. This recipe also makes a great soup, simply add more water at the soaking stage.

BARLEY, LEEK AND NETTLE 'RISOTTO'

Serves 6:
2 cups barley, soaked in 5-6 cups water or 8-9 cups for a soup.
1-2 cups of young nettle leaves
2 celery sticks, diced
1 onion, diced
1 carrot, diced
2 leeks, sliced on diagonal
1 cup wild garlic leaves
2 tbsp sweet white miso
1 tbsp tahini
1 tbsp ume paste

Saute the onion carrot and celery in 1 tbsp oil with 1/2 tsp salt. Add the barley with the soaking water and cook on a low heat for 30 minutes. Add the leek and nettles, with a little extra water if needed, and cook for 10 more minutes. Add the wild garlic leaves, and allow them to wilt into the dish; mix the sweet miso, tahini and ume paste together to blend well, and stir in well, garnish with primrose, or chopped herbs, and serve.

A delicious savoury pancake that is light, yet satisfying. It's good to lightly steam the vegetables first before putting them in the mixture. For cooking the pancakes, use a stainless frying pan and good quality oil.

SPRING VEGETABLE PANCAKES

Makes 10-12 pancakes:
2 cups wholemeal spelt flour
or for gluten free 1 cup buckwheat
and 1 cup chickpea
1 egg (optional)
2 cups oat milk
1 tsp salt
1 tbsp lemon juice
Vegetables:
6 asparagus halved length ways
1 small carrot sliced in batons
1 small leek cut in thin diagonal rings
6 purple sprouting broccoli, halved
length ways

Mix the ingredients for the pancake batter and leave to rest whilst preparing the vegetables. Steam the vegetables until they are al dente, about 3-4 minutes, refresh with cold water. Add into the batter, stirring to combine.
Heat a tsp oil in a frying pan for each pancake and cook them for about 2 minutes on each side. Enjoy with tofu sour cream, p.67

GREEN SPLIT PEA DAHL

Spilt peas are nutritious and rich in protein, a great addition to a plant based diet. This is a simple, delicious recipe that is quick and easy to prepare, but also incredibly tasty.

Serves 4:
1 cup split peas, soaked for 1/2 hr.
3 cups water
1/2 tsp turmeric
1/2 cup dulse
1/2 tsp salt
2-3 tsp oil
2 tbsp chopped coriander
1/2 cup wild garlic leaves, optional
1 tsp garam masala
1 tbsp white miso
Juice 1/2 lemon

Drain the soaked split peas, and add to a pan with the 3 cups of water, bring to boil and skim any froth away. add the dulse, salt & tumeric' then cover, turn to a low heat, using a flame spreader if you have one, and cook for 1 hour. When the split peas are cooked, quickly fry the garam masala in the oil, add the herbs and then stir into the dahl with the sweet miso and lemon
juice to taste.

'PRESSED' COLESLAW SALAD

Pressed salads are a fabulous addition to the diet, especially as a cleansing opening food for spring time or an uplifting energy. I love coleslaw, it can make a spring or summer meal really come alive. Pressed salads are also called quick pickles, with some of the health benefits of longer pickles like sauerkraut. The digestive bacteria are activated, nutritional content increased, and the body is more easily able to digest the raw foods.

Serves 4-6 as a side dish:
1/2 small white cabbage, finely sliced
1/2 large red or white onion, finely sliced
1 large carrot, grated or thin julienne
handful of chives, chopped
1 tsp salt
2 tbsp tahini dressing or vegan mayo

Knead the salt into the vegetables. Then using a salad press, or a bowl with plate and heavy weight, press the cabbage onions and carrots for about 1 hour. The juices should run from the vegetables. Once they are ready, add the chives and the dressing or mayo, and serve.

TEMPEH AND SAUERKRAUT

Tempeh is very nutritious and a classic dish from Indonesia. Tempeh's fermented quality makes it a great protein choice for spring, as fermented foods link with the opening alive energy we can feel around us.

1 8 oz block organic tempeh
1-2 cups water
2 tbsp shoyu
1" ginger piece cut into slices
1 large onion, cut into thin half moons
1/2 tsp salt
3 tbsp olive oil
1 cup sauerkraut
1 tbsp mustard

Prepare the tempeh by simmering it in a small covered pan with the water, shoyu and ginger for 25-30 minutes. Sauté the onion in 1 tbsp of the olive oil with the salt for 10-15 minutes until it is translucent and soft. Cut the tempeh into squares, and fry in a pan with the remaining oil until crispy; add to the onions with the remaining cooking water from the tempeh, about half a cup is good. Add the sauerkraut and mustard, and cook for 5 minutes to combine the flavours. Serve warm, with parsley as an optional garnish.

SWEET AND SOUR VEGETABLES

This is a light tasty spring dish, with the vinegar making it zesty and alive. Add tempeh or fish to make it a more substantial meal.

1 leek, sliced thin on a diagonal
1 carrot cut into diagonal batons
6 radish, sliced thin on a diagonal
1 small kohlrabi cut into batons
6 heads of purple sprouting broccoli, cut in half length ways
1 tbsp arrowroot, dissolved in a little water
1/2 packet udon noodles (use buckwheat for gluten free)
2 tbsp rice or apple cyder vinegar
2 tbsp ume plum seasoning
1 tbsp apple concentrate

Cook the noodles until al dente. Refresh and put to one side. Water saute the vegetables by placing vegetables in a wok with 1/2 cup of water in the bottom. Start with the carrots, leeks and kohlrabi, cooking for 5 minutes; add the radish and broccoli and cook for a further 5 minutes. Add another 1/2-1 cup of water to the cooked vegetables, together with the seasonings, and stir in the arrowroot until thickened. Add the noodles and warm through, or serve the vegetables on top of the noodles.

This makes a lovely breakfast or light supper. Tofu's delicate flavour and light texture blends well with the opening magic of spring. Serve this as a breakfast or light lunch with noodles or homemade bread..

SCRAMBLED TOFU

1 leek, cut into fine strips
1 carrots, grated
1 tbsp olive oil
1-2 tbsp spring herbs, chopped
1 tbsp ume vinegar
1 tbsp lemon juice
1 large block tofu, crumbled (about 450g)
Black pepper to taste

Heat the olive oil in a pan. Add the leeks and carrots, and sauté slowly for 10 minutes. Add the tofu and fry for another 5 minutes. Add the seasonings and herbs to your tofu and serve, topped with wilted spring greens, wild garlic, spinach or other favourite edible greens.

STEAMED SODABREAD

Reducing baked flour is a great way to allow the opening energy of spring. This bread is a great alternative that is tasty yet lighter than baked bread. Soda bread is normally made with soured milk. This is a vegan version, using lemon to trigger the same effect as the milk.

3 cups wholemeal spelt flour
2 1/2 cups barley flour
2 cups oat milk
Juice half a lemon
1 heaped tsp bicarbonate of soda

Mix all the ingredients together to form a dough. Form into a circular loaf and place in a cake tin. Place in a large pan with a bowl, or another cake tin, upside down on the bottom to lift the bread tin; fill with a few inches of water, cover and steam for 45 minutes, remove from tin and allow to cool.

1 - Remove any old dry outer leaves and cut the dry stem off neaty Finely slice the cabbage, including the core.

3 - Place something heavy on top to hold everything in place as it ferments. All the cabbage must be under the juice or it will not work. Allow to stand in a warm room for 7-10 days.

5 - Continue massaging until the cabbage is sitting in plenty of juice, enough to cover once it is pushed down. This takes about 15 minutes.

2 - Place the sliced cabbage in a large bowl and add the salt. Begin to massage the cabbage so the juice releases, osmosis.

4 - Find a plate or something similar (I made a cirle from slate) that fits really well inside your crock. Push it down hard so that all the cabbage is under the juice.

6 - Place the cabbage and its juice in a lareg crock or glass jar.

STEP BY STEP: SAUERKRAUT

Sauerkraut meaning 'Sour Cabbage' boasts an array of health benefits. I also find it a great condiment and flavour to a meal, and a good way to include Tree energy in the colder months. The fermentation process produces beneficial probiotics, including Lactobacillus acidophilus, making sauerkraut the healthiest probiotic on the market. Cabbage, by itself, offers a number of health benefits, but the fermentation process increases the nutrients making sauerkraut even more nutritious than the original cabbage itself. Once fermented, this recipe will give you about 4 jars of sauerkraut.

Ingredients:
2 large white cabbages
2 tbsp salt

Pickling vegetables increases vitamin content and produces good bacteria for the gut. The opening energy of fermented vegetables is also opening and cleansing for the liver. When radish come into season, it's great to pickle them, I find them a good vegetable to pickle. Make sure you choose radish of a similar size.

PICKLED RADISHES

Make a brine by boiling 1l of water and stirring in 1 tbsp salt. Allow to cool. Top and tail 2-3 cups of radish and pack them into a jar, cover with the cooled brine, making sure all the radish are under the liquid. You may not use the whole litre, save leftovers for another pickle. Use another jar that fits inside to hold the radish down if needed. Place the jar in shaded place in your kitchen and leave to ferment for approx 4-6 days, the time needed will depend on the room temperature. Once fermented, they will taste zingy and alive; keep refrigerated.

Foraging for new season, wild leaves is in itself a great way to nourish the element of Tree. Gather what you have around you, adding any other favourite herbs and leaves too.

WILD LEAF SALAD

Winter cress, hawthorn leaves, beech leaves, ladies mantle, dandelion leaves, wild garlic, primrose flowers, jack by the hedge, plantain flowers heads, sorrel, watercress, rocket, lemon balm, chives or other garden herbs.

Add your chosen foraged leaves to a salad with grated carrots, finely sliced red cabbage and/or sliced radishes. Serve with a zesty dressing, see P:66

I love spring especially when the purple sprouting broccoli arrives. Water sautéing is a great way to lightly cook vegetables, and adding a handful of wild greens to wilt into this dish adds excitement, flavour and nutrition.

WATER SAUTEED PURPLE SPROUTING BROCCOLI AND WILD SPRING GREENS

Serves 4 as side dish:
16 thin heads of purple sprouting broccoli (or 8 thick halved)
2 cups wild spring greens: dandelion leaves, plantain leaves, wild garlic, ground elder
Dressing: 1 tbsp apple concentrate, 1 tbsp apple cider vinegar, 1/2 tbsp mustard, 1 tbsp olive oil, black pepper to taste

Add 1/4 cup water to a hot wok and water saute the broccoli for 5 mins, add the wild greens, cook for another couple of minutes, adding a little extra water if needed. Pour the dressing on top and serve.

Refreshing, opening and light, this tasty salad is a lovely spring time side dish, great for gently cleansing the body. Fresh chives out the garden, or your favourite spring herbs, can be added for extra flavours.

CUCUMBER MOOLI AND SAUERKRAUT SALAD

1 cup grated cucumber
1 cup grated mooli or kohl rabi
1 cup sauerkraut
1 tbsp fresh chives

Mix the cucumber and mooli, gently rub in the sauerkraut blending all three ingredients together. Add spring herbs and season to taste.

DRESSINGS

Using a variety of seasonings, we can create a tangy zesty interest into our meal, balancing other flavours and elements in the meal. I have given here some of my favourite dressings, but also, it's fun to play yourself creating great flavours with different seasonings; choose from:

dijon mustard	barley miso
whole grain mustard	herbs
apple concentrate	chilli
lemon juice	apple cider vinegar
ume vinegar	brown rice vinegar
ume puree	olive oil
garlic	sesame oil
shoyu	black pepper
sweet miso	herb salt
rice syrup	pumpkin seed paste
tahini	almond butter

MUSTARD DRESSING

1 tbsp dijon mustard
1 tbsp wholegrain mustard
1 tbsp lemon juice
1 tbsp olive oil
1 tbsp rice syrup

UME DRESSING

1 tbsp ume vinegar
1 tbsp rice vinegar
1 tbsp apple concentrate
1 tbsp sweet miso (optional)

TAHINI DRESSING

1 tbsp tahini
2 tbsp lemon
1 tbsp olive oil
1 tbsp sweet msio
1 tbsp water (optional)

TOFU SOUR CREAM

1 cup organic tofu, about 200g
Juice from 1 small lemon
4 tbsp olive oil
2 spring onions, chopped
1 tbsp water
2 tbsp ume seasoning
Blend all ingredients in a blender

PESTO DRESSING

1 tbsp pesto
1 tbsp lemon juice
2 tbsp olive oil

Chutney is a great way to harness spring energy and take it through the year. Using seasonal rhubarb gives a zingy mouth watering chutney. Make sure you use a good quality vinegar, with Mother.

RHUBARB CHUTNEY

3/4 cups dates, chopped
1/2 cup apricots, chopped
3-4 eating apples, peeled cored and diced in 1cm pieces
2 star anise
1 stick cinnamon
1 1/2 cups apple cider vinegar
3 sticks rhubarb (no leaves), chopped
into 1cm pieces

Place all the ingredients in a pan and bring to the boil. Turn down to a very low heat, cover and simmer for 1 1/2 to 2 hours. Remove the cinnamon and star anise and place the chutney in kilners jars; you will get about 2 jars of chutney from this recipe. Store in the fridge.

PICKLED WILD GARLIC FLOWERS

These are a great delight that can take spring energy through the year. The flavour is strong and it makes for a nice condiment like sauerkraut. The inspiration for doing this was brought to me by my foraging friend, Andrew Tomlinson. The recipe calls for wild garlic flowers just before they have opened, so watch out for that moment just before bloom. Using a good quality vinegar is also important to me, I choose apple cider vinegar with Mother.

4 cups garlic flowers
2 cup apple cider vinegar

Place the flowers and garlic in a kilner jar. Make sure all the flowers are underneath the vinegar, I use a jar on top to ensure this. Leave in a dark place to pickle for at least one week. Store in the fridge.

BUCKWHEAT & OAT PANCAKES

Pancakes use flour but have a lighter energy than baking bread, which suits well with the energy of spring. Buckwheat is a strong grain perfect for pancakes. You can make this recipe gluten free by using gluten free oats; and it can also be vegan as you don't need to use an egg, although the pancakes will be more delicate if you don't. For a great spring pancake, serve these for breakfast, or as a desert, with lemon and rice syrup, or savoury with hummus and sauerkraut.

Makes 10-12 pancakes:
1 1/2 cup buckwheat flour
1 cup porridge oats
1 cup oat milk
2 cups water
1 tbsp rice syrup
1 egg (optional)
1 tsp of salt
Extra oil for frying

Place the flour, salt and oats in a large bowl. Combine the wet ingredients. Pour over the dry mixture, stir to combine, and then leave to soak for 15-20 minutes. Blend until smooth if desired; I sometimes leave this part out for a textured pancake. Coat the bottom of a frying pan with a tsp of oil and heat, do not allow oil to smoke. Pour in a ladle full of the batter and fry on a medium heat for about one minute. Flip over and cook on the other side for one minute, serve warm.

A light, quick and simple porridge, toasting the oats before you add the water gives a nutty deeper flavour to your porridge. Serve with toasted seeds and nori and edible spring flowers, here I have added gorse bush flowers, a lovely edible flower in abundance in the Cumbrian spring.

ROLLED OAT PORRIDGE

Serves 4-6:
2 cups rolled oats
5 cups water
1/2 cup sultanas
1/2 sheet nori, cut into small strips
Pinch of salt

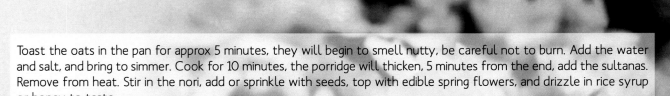

Toast the oats in the pan for approx 5 minutes, they will begin to smell nutty, be careful not to burn. Add the water and salt, and bring to simmer. Cook for 10 minutes, the porridge will thicken, 5 minutes from the end, add the sultanas. Remove from heat. Stir in the nori, add or sprinkle with seeds, top with edible spring flowers, and drizzle in rice syrup or honey to taste.

PRIMROSE AND LEMON KANTEN

It's great to use spring nature in a desert. I adore the energy of primroses, 'the first rose'; even though, they are not closely related, they have a similar energy to roses. It's great as they appear in the woodlands at Sunny Brow, as I know spring arrived and the new cycle is beginning. Their energy and light yellow colour opens and touches the heart.

Serves 4:
2 1/2 cups of water
1/2 cup apple concentrate
3 level tbsp agar flakes
1 tsp grated lemon rind
2 tbsp lemon juice
20 wild primroses

Bring the water, lemon and agar to the boil and simmer for 5-8 mins until all the agar has dissolved. Remove from heat and add the apple concentrate. Allow to cool slightly and pour into small cups or glasses. Add the primroses to the top and leave to cool and set.

Rhubarb is a sour fruit, perfect for nourishing Tree energy. It's really easy to grow too and has been a part of my life since childhood. The first stems appear in spring and are beautifully
fresh and tart. Don't use the leaf part, it's toxic, just the pink stem.

RHUBARB WITH HEMP CREAM

Makes 4:
For the Rhubarb:
4-6 stems of rhubarb, chopped into 1 cm pieces
6-8 apricots, soaked in 1/2 cup water
for 30 mins, and chopped into pieces
1/2 teaspoon salt
2-3 tbsp apple concentrate depending on
sweetness of rhubarb
1 tbsp arrowroot or kuzu, diluted in a little water

For the hemp cream:
1 1/2 cups hulled hemp seeds
1 tsp vanilla essence
1/2 cup oat or rice milk
3 tbsp rice syrup

Cook the rhubarb and apricots in the soaking water until soft, about 5-6 minutes. sweeten with the apple concentrate, add salt, and stir in the arrowroot or kuzu to thicken. Allow to cool. Blend together the hemp cream ingredients until smooth and sweet. Pour the fruit into nice glasses and top with the hemp cream; place in the fridge to chill for at least 1/2 hour. Garnish with spring flowers to serve.

LEMON MOUSSE

Simple to prepare, light and fluffy; this lemon mousse is a winner for all the family, and an opening yet satisfying desert.

Makes 4:
1 cup amazake
1 cup oat milk
Juice & zest from a lemon
1 tbsp tahini
2 tbsp rice syrup
1 tbsp arrowroot
1 tbsp kuzu
Pinch salt

Warm the amazake, oat milk, tahini and lemon. Dissolve the kuzu and arrowroot in 2 tbsp of water; and add stirring vigourously for 2-3 minutes until the mixture has thickened. Remove from the heat and add the sweetener and pinch of salt . Chill in the fridge and serve, topped with nuts, sunflower seeds, wild flowers and/or lemon zest.

Spring is about fertility and new life, so eggs are a big part of this. I always make alternative chocolate eggs at Easter for my children so they don't miss out. My eldest son Roan had the idea that our chocolate eggs should be in spring section of this book.

CACAO CHOC
MINI EGGS

1/4 cup cacao powder
1/4 cup cocoa powder
100g cacao butter
1 tsp vanilla essence
3/4 cup brown rice syrup
Pinch salt

Melt the butter in a small pan over a low heat. Add the salt. Combine and whisk in the powders. Remove from heat and add the syrup and vanilla.
Pour into mini egg moulds, which come in half egg shapes. Cool in the fridge for 1 hour. We either wrap two halves together in coloured foil or to make whole mini eggs melt the flat side of one half egg, in a little boiling water in a hot pan and quickly fix together with another half. Delicious.

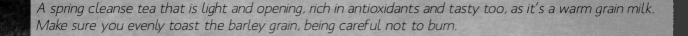

A spring cleanse tea that is light and opening, rich in antioxidants and tasty too, as it's a warm grain milk. Make sure you evenly toast the barley grain, being careful not to burn.

BARLEY TEA

Serves 2-3:
1/2 cup barley grain
4 cups water

Begin by toasting the barley slowly in a small pan until it is browning and smells nutty. It can take about 5-10 minutes on a very low flame, make sure you shake or stir for even toasting and to prevent burning. Add the water, cover and simmer for 20 minutes. Pour into individual cups and sweeten to taste with the rice or barley syrup.

NETTLE AND LEMON INFUSION

Cleanse the body with this special infusion, a great way to embrace spring. Use the nettle hearts from the first spring nettles for maximum taste and cleanse. This infusion is delicious hot or cold; the longer you leave the nettles to steep, the more nutritious it becomes.

Serves 3-4:
2 cup fresh nettle hearts
2 lemon slices
3-4 tsp rice syrup or honey
3 cups water

Boil the water in a pan, add the nettles and bring to the boil for a couple of minutes. Remove from the heat and pour into a tea pot with the lemon or add the lemon into the pan; allow to steep for 5-10 minutes. If desired, add 1 tsp sweetener per cup. Enjoy.

SUMMER

AND THE ELEMENT OF FIRE

The transition between spring and summer is one of my favourite times of year. There is such freshness in the air, promise blossom and bloom. It's great to really connect to this energy of blossoming, I find it really helps me to come into the fullness of my own flow creativity and manifestation. The energy rises even higher than in spring and this energy opens the nature around us. Trees come into fullness with their amazing canopies of leaves. Plants begin to burst into their own fullness with an array of beautiful flowers.

In June, the beginning of summer is here, it is a fantastic month when the newly bloomed energy and plants are alive and fresh. The world is warmer and brighter; the days are long with plenty of sunlight. The breath of heaven and earth mingles to create an alchemy of creativity, bloom and fruit; this is a time for outward expression of who we are, and like the flower, we can embody all that we are and take it out into the world.

In the kitchen, summer is about great produce from our garden and our local farmers' vegetable boxes, and many wild herbs and flowers; using this abundance in my cooking is a real joy. The varying colours are amazing, different reds, pinks, yellows, greens, everything is expressing itself and we get to benefit from this in what we eat and in how we are in ourselves.

Summer solstice on, or around, the 21st June, is the time to celebrate the sun at its height. The day is at its longest, the night at its shortest. It is a time to embrace life in its fullness. But it is also the shift to energy coming inwards again. The rising energy stops as the sun reaches its peak, and from here, it settles towards an incoming again. Don't forget to still stay connected to the roots in this season; they serve to give you the nourishment to be out in the world. Summer can be a busy vibrant time, use the foods in this book to make sure you don't forget the body. If you feel imbalanced, you can also connect to the oak tree whose roots equal its canopy; use this energy to be up and outward but rooted too.

In season:
Kohl rabi, carrots, chard, spinach, endive, peas, parsley, basil, coriander, runner beans, salad onions, fennel, radishes, herbs, lemon balm, red berries, summer cauliflowers, lettuces, broad beans, rhubarb, strawberries and raspberries, red currants, summer squashes, courgettes, tomatoes, peppers.

In the wild:
Elderflowers, meadowsweet, sweet cicely, wild strawberries, wild raspberries, red clover, wild rose, dandelion, wild herbs, such as, water mint, cow parsley (wild chervil), herb robert, lemon balm, borage, thyme, wild fennel, hawthorn flowers.

80

The element of Fire is dynamic and bold, with heat and intensity. It is full of vitality, aliveness, colour, passion and love. It is exciting and transformative. It is laughter and joy. It is the peak of power and action. The energy of the sun or flames of a fire burn, warm and nourish, and without the sun, there would be no life.

The organs related to this element are heart and small intestine. Just as the sun gives the rhythm to our life as it rises and falls each day, our hearts form the beat in our body and this pulse runs the blood through our veins. Fire is a powerful element of love and life in fullness. Our bodies hold the energy of the Fire, we are fire, we are warmth, we are love. A person with strong fire energy will stride confidently into social situations, they can easily open their hearts with laughter, joy, family and friends. We must work to balance this element; it holds a strong intense energy within the cycle and can easily be tipped off centre.

If we do not have enough Fire, we can get cold in body and heart, with no fire, it can get cold inside; poor circulation, cold extremities, varicose veins, hemorrhoids, heart burn, lack of joy and digestive problems if the digestive fire is weak. Get out in the sun and warm the body. Eat the Fire foods from this section to bring excitement and enliven the body. Eat opening salads, wild flowers, tomatoes, peppers and red berries.

If we have too much Fire, we risk 'burning out',or becoming overly 'buzzy', with symptoms such as hot flushes, restlessness, hyperactivity and inappropriate laughter. To balance, we can look to the food preparation in the Water and Metal sections, reduce your Fire by finding calm ways to relax, spend more inward time, and maybe a few less social engagements to reduce the intensity of the Fire. Avoid the Fire foods, as these will make you buzzier.

Things to nourish Fire energy:
opening foods and salads, juicing, lettuce, bitter greens, bitter flavours, chicory, dandelion, quick cooking, stir frying, raw foods, chilli, sunshine, summer, falling in love, dancing, wild flowers & foods that grow in summer, tomatoes, peppers and red berries.

The dough for the bottom of this pizza comes from a Spanish influence, bought to me by a lovely Spanish helper who was a great cook; it's a nice alternative to an Italian style base. We eat this pizza all year, varying the toppings according to what's in season! For this book, I've put it in the summer, as I often use tomatoes for the sauce, and summer veggies and herbs to create a light and very yummy pizza. When cooking this, you must get your oven and pizza stone really hot to cook it nice and quick. The quantities here will give you two large pizzas.

SUMMER PIZZA

Dough:
6 1/2 cups flour
3/4 cup olive oil
1 1/2 cups ale
1 tsp salt
Sauce:
1/2 small squash
1 large carrot
2 tins tomatoes
1/2 cup water

Topping:
250g tofu, crumbled
1 tbsp white miso
1/2 tbsp ume purée
1/2 tbsp tahini
1/2 cup olive, chopped
1 cup cherry tomatoes, halved
1 red pepper
1 tbsp fresh basil

Heat the oven to 220 degrees C.
Roast the pepper whole for 20 minutes, until charred; cool, deseed, peel and slice into strips. Mix the miso, ume and tahini together well and combine with the crumbled tofu. To prepare the sauce, grate the carrots and squash and sauté with 2 tbsp oil and a tsp of salt for 10 minutes. Add the tomato with the water, cover and cook for 20 minutes on a low heat. Blend to get a smooth sauce. To prepare the dough, mix the oil and ale, and combine with the flour and salt in a large bowl. roll the dough approximately 1cm thick to fit a pizza stone. Heat the pizza stone or a baking tray, then place the rolled out dough on top, spread with the sauce, and scatter the tofu, red pepper, tomatoes and olives. Bake in the hot oven for 10-15 minutes, adding the fresh basil leaves on top, once cooked.

A light yet satisfying soup, using fresh seasonal broccoli, garden peas and mint if available. The tasty topping adds the exciting essence of the Fire element.

BROCCOLI, PEA AND MINT SOUP

For the soup, serves 4-5:
1 broccoli head, chopped into florets
3 cups fresh or frozen peas
1 leek, chopped into rounds
2 small potato or 1/2 celeriac, cubed
Handful dulse seaweed
1 cup of fresh spinach leaves
2-3 tbsp fresh mint
2 tbsp olive oil
2 tbsp sweet miso

6 cups water
1 cup oat cream
For the salsa:
1 red pepper, finely diced
2 spring onions, finely diced
1 tsp chilli flakes (optional)
juice 1/2 lime
1 tbsp olive
2 tsp ume vinegar

Add the leek, potato and broccoli to a pan and cover with the water. Bring to the boil and simmer for 10 minutes. Add the peas and dulse and simmer for 5 more minutes. Blend with the herbs, oil, cream and miso. Mix the salsa ingredients together and serve on the top of each individual soup, garnished with mint.

This is a quick and easy dish to prepare, and it's tasty too. In summer, it's enjoyable to include spices and herbs; they have an expansive energy that suits the energy of warmer months.

RED LENTIL DAHL

Serves 4:
1 onion, diced
2 cups red lentils
6 cups water or stock
2 tsp ground cumin
1 tsp salt
1 tbsp coconut oil
Handful of dulse seaweed
2" finely chopped ginger
1-2 cloves garlic
1 chilli (optional)
1-2 tbsp fresh coriander

Saute onions, garlic, ginger and chilli if using, with the oil, salt and cumin, on a low heat for 10 minutes. Add the lentils and saute for 2-3 minutes more. Add water, or stock, and dulse, and cook slowly with a flame spreader for 20-30 minutes. Stir in coriander, and serve.

WILD AND RED CAMARGUE RICE SALAD

This makes a fabulous summer lunch, light supper, or side dish for a bigger meal. Red rice is light and nutty, black wild rice is hearty and nutritious; you can buy them in a mix with long grain rice, which is a great combination for a summer rice dish.

Serves 4-6:
1 cup mixed wild, red and long grain rice
2 spring onions, finely sliced on diagonal
1/2 avocado, finely sliced
4 radish, finely sliced on diagonal
1/4 cucumber, halved and finely sliced
on diagonal
1 stick celery, finely sliced on diagonal
1 tomato chopped (optional)
1/2 nori sheet, cut into thin short pieces
1/2 cup toasted pumpkin and sunflower
seeds
1 lemon juice and rind
1 tbsp ume vinegar
1 tbsp olive oil

Cook the rice in 2 cups water using a very low heat, and flame spreader if you have one, for about 45 minutes. All the water should be absorbed, leaving perfect rice. When it is cooked, cool quickly; for this, I use a metal bowl in a larger bowl of cold water. While the rice is cooking, place the spring onion, radish and celery in a salad press, with the ume vinegar, for 1/2 hour. Add the cucumber and press for a further 10 minutes. An alternative here is that you can just add the raw salads without pressing. When the rice is cooled, mix together all of the ingredients and the dressing, and serve.

STAFFORDSHIRE OATCAKES WITH AUBERGINE & CUMIN SEEDS

The recipe for these oatcakes was passed on to me by a very good friend and neighbour, it was her grandmother's recipe so credit here to Jane Archebold, who was an amazing cook. Staffordshire oatcakes are very similar to pancakes but with a heartier texture that is tasty and enjoyable with sweet or savoury fillings.

Makes 12-14 pancakes:
2 cups porridge oats
2 1/2 cups flour (I use wholemeal spelt)
1 1/2 cups oat milk
2 1/2 cups warm water
2 tsp yeast
1 tsp salt
For the Aubergine:
2 aubergine, diced
1 large red or white onion, diced
1 tsp cumin seeds
1-2 tbsp olive oil
1 tsp salt
1 red chilli sliced finely
1 tbsp fresh coriander

Mix all the dry ingredients for the oatcakes. Mix the wet ingredients and add the yeast. Blend the wet and dry together to form a batter, and leave for 15 minutes. Fry like pancakes; heat a tsp oil in a pan and cook for 1-1 1/2 minutes on each side.

Fry the onion and aubergine with the spices and salt until soft, about 15 minutes. Add the coriander.

To serve: Fill the pancakes with a dahl p.84, p.87 or hummus p.119, add aubergine mixture on top and roll. .

This yummy dahl dish is inspired by ayuvedic cooking; it is grounding but uplifting too, and the chilli is optional so omit if you want to go for more grounding than uplifting. Moong dahl is split mung bean..

MOONG DAHL WITH SWEET POTATO

1 1/2 cups moong dahl
4 1/2 cups water or stock
1 large onion, diced
2 cups (about 1 large) sweet potatoes,
cut into 1cm cubes
1/2 tsp ground coriander
1/2 tsp turmeric
1-2 cloves garlic, cut finely
1" ginger, cut finely
1 tsp cumin
1 tsp chilli
1 tsp salt
2 tbsp coconut oil
1 tbsp fresh coriander, chopped finely

Saute the onions in the coconut oil, with the spices and salt, for 5 minutes. Add the moong dahl and stir fry for a couple more minutes. Add the water and bring to the boil; cover and cook for 25 minutes on a low heat. Stir in the coriander and leave to infuse.

Serve with rice or chappatis.

PASTA EL ERB

I had a great Italian guy, Stephano, stay with me last year who was a good chef; he gave me lots of tips of how to cook tasty pasta dishes. Here is one of our creations, based on an Italian classic 'pasta el erb', translates as pasta with herbs.

Serves 6:
3 cup garden herbs...
basil, parsley, mint, thyme, sage, rocket, coriander, and/or marjoram
1/2 cup almonds or sunflower seeds, toasted
1/2 cup olive oil.
1 tbsp sweet miso
1 tbsp ume paste
1 cup cherry tomatoes, halved
1 tbsp balsamic vinegar
1 packet wholemeal pasta, cooked to al dente and cooled.

Make the pesto using your selection of garden herbs and rocket, blend together with the almonds, olive oil and seasonings. Add to your al dente pasta once it has cooled, adding more olive oil if needed to combine pasta and sauce. Sear the cherry tomatoes with some olive oil in a hot pan. Add a tbsp of balsamic vinegar. Serve with the pasta.

This is a really yummy variation of hummus that is creamy and light. I serve it with summer salads or as a dip with crunchy crudite.

BUTTERBEAN PUREE

1 cup dried butter beans
1 4-6" piece kombu
2 tbsp olive oil
1 lemon juiced
1 tbsp ume paste

Soak butterbeans in plenty of water and leave to soak over night. Refresh the water, add the kombu and bring to the boil. Cover and simmer until cooked, about 50 minutes-1 hour, until the beans are soft. Drain the beans, blend with olive oil, lemon juice and ume paste. Taste and add more seasonings if needed.

This is a perfect summer fish dish, light and nutritious, cooked over a hot flame. I always find a nice piece of fish, really satisfying in the summer; serving it with an opening salsa verde allows a nice balance of energy and flavours. I often serve this on a bed of nori which is very delicious with the fish.

SEA BASS WITH SALSA VERDE

Serves 4:
4 fillets sea bass
For the salsa verde:
1 tbsp capers
4 anchovies
1 tbsp mustard
2 cups chopped herbs,
coriander, parsley, basil, mint
2 tbsp olive oil

Blend together the ingredients for the salsa. Rub the 4 sea bass fillets with 1-2 tsp of olive oil each and a pinch of salt. Heat a griddle or frying pan until hot and sear the fish on each side for about 2 minutes. Season with some black pepper, and serve with the salsa verde.

SUMMER CASSEROLE

In the summer, quick, lighter cooking is ideal for the body. When preparing this stew, cutting the vegetables into small dices will ensure the dish can be cooked in a short time. Use whatever vegetables are available to you, I have put some recommended ones here, but stews are very flexible, so feel free to experiment with other summer vegetables too.

1 red onion
2 small new season carrots, diced
1 fennel, diced
1 red pepper, diced
1/2 tsp salt
1/2 cup broadbeans, peeled
8 radish quartered
1 leek, diced
1 large courgette, diced
1 cup cooked butter or cannelini beans
2 cups vegetable stock
1 tsp fennel seeds
2 tbsp lemon juice
1 tbsp ume vinegar
1 tbsp sweet miso.
2 tbsp Summer herbs, wild or garden.

Saute the carrots, fennel, pepper and red onion in 1 tbsp oil, with the salt and fennel seeds, for 5 minutes; add the rest of the vegetables and combine. Add the stock and bring to the boil; turn down to a simmer and cook for 10 minutes. Add the beans and simmer for another 5-10 minutes until the vegetables are soft. Add the herbs, lemon juice, ume vinegar and sweet miso. Serve with a light grain dish and/or green salad leaves.

RATATOUILLE

A fantastic classic recipe that was inspired by one of my French helpers. She taught me the classic French way as taught to her by her mum, and it is actually very straight forward. I also found out that one traditional way to serve it is warm with rice.

1 large onion, cut into chunks
1 red pepper, cut into chunks
1 medium aubergine, cut into chunks
2 courgettes, cut into chunks
6 ripe tomatoes, cut into chunks or 1 tin tomatoes
1 tbsp olive oil
1 tbsp balsamic vinegar
1 tsp salt
1 tbsp parsley
black pepper and shoyu to taste

Saute the onions in the olive oil with the salt, for about 5 minutes. Add all of the remaining ingredients, except the parsley, and bring to simmer. Cover and cook on a low heat for about 30 minutes or until all the vegetables are soft. Add the parsley, and allow to rest. Season to taste with black pepper and shoyu. We serve it with wholegrain brown rice, or in a wrap or pancake.

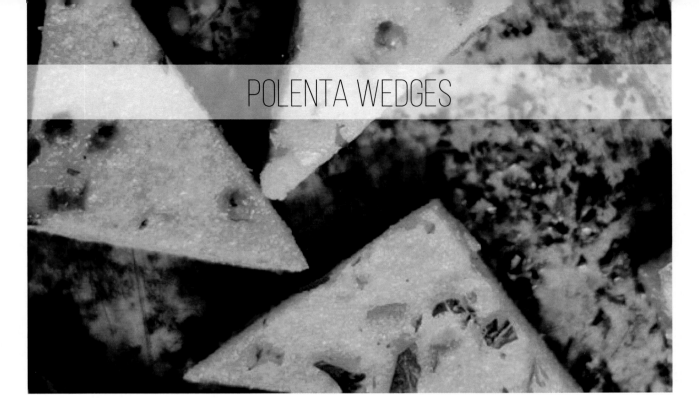

POLENTA WEDGES

A great side dish for any meal and great for picnics. The vegetables give a nice addition and flavour to the polenta, red pepper can be nice too, but also you can exclude them if you wish, just making plain polenta. Polenta is great served with ratatoullie, chilli, or a simple tomato or 'no tomato' sauce.

Serves 4-6 as a side dish:
1 1/2 cups polenta
4 1/2 cups water
1 tbsp boullion
1/2 cup peas
1 small onion, diced
1 small carrot, diced
1 tbsp olive oil
1 tsp salt
Extra oil to fry or bake

Saute the onion and carrot with the oil and salt for about 5 minutes until soft, add the peas, and cook through. Add the polenta and stir; add the water and bring to the boil. Cook for 5 minutes, stirring well as the polenta thickens. Pour into a medium baking tray and allow to cool. Cut into squares or triangles and shallow fry, or bake in a preheated oven at 200 degrees C, until crispy.

A lovely summer dish. The mix of coloured vegetables means it is full of excitement and spark. At Sunny Brow, we serve it with salad, and rice or polenta. Cutting the vegetables roughly the same size as the beans will blend the ingredients together in a lovely rainbow array.

RAINBOW CHILLI

Serves 4-6:
2 carrots, diced
1/2 small squash, diced
1 red pepper, diced
1 yellow pepper, diced
1 bulb fennel, diced
1 onion, diced
2 sticks celery, diced
1 courgette, diced
2 large tomatoes diced
1 1/2 cups cooked kidney beans
2 cloves garlic, chopped finely
1 tbsp herbs, parsley or coriander,
chopped finely
2 tsp ground cumin
1" piece ginger, finely chopped
1-2 tsp dried chilli flakes
1 tbsp shoyu

Saute onions, garlic, ginger and chilli with the salt and cumin on a low heat for 5 minutes. Add the hard vegetables and cook for 5 more minutes. Add 1 1/2 cups water and bring to boil. Cover and simmer for 15-20 minutes. Add the courgette, tomatoes and beans; add the shoyu and cook for 5 more minutes. Stir in the herbs, and serve.

BLACKBEAN TORTILLA WRAPS WITH AVOCADO, SALSA & TOFU SOUR CREAM

This is a family favourite and winner dinner that never fails to please. I love the use of hearty dark black beans from the Water element combined with some summery magic of tomato, cucumber, avocado and corriander.

Serves 4-6:
For the black beans: see recipe on p 183
For the Salsa:
3 tomatoes, diced
1 chilli, diced
1/2 cucumber, diced
1 tbsp fresh coriander, chopped finely
For the Avocado puree:
2 avocados
2 tbsp lemon juice
1 clove garlic
1 tbsp chopped coriander
For the tofu sour cream: see p.67
For the tortilla wraps, makes 12-14 :
3 1/2 cups wholemeal flour
4 tbsp oil
1 tsp baking powder
1 tsp salt
3/4 cup warm water

For the black beans, make sure you use the 3:1 water bean ratio and that all the water has cooked away, leaving you with thick black beans.
For the salsa, mix all the ingredients together with optional 1 tbps olive oil and allow flavours to infuse.
Blend the ingredients for the avocado puree and place one avocado stone in the middle, which helps to prevent browning.
Mix all dry ingredients for the tortillas and then rub in the oil. Mix in the water forming into a soft dough ball. Split into 12-14 balls, rolling each out into a circle and cooking in a dry frying pan, on a medium heat for about 1 minute on each side.
To serve, place some black beans, salsa, tofu sour cream and avocado puree in the middle of a tortilla and fold over to form a wrap or roll. Delicious.

This super dish is great for fire energy as chicory is particularly bitter, I designed it for the Fire element cooking session that's part of my 5 seasons cookery course. Using the wild flowers adds to the feel and energy of summer. This photograph was actually taken on the cookery day, so I must give credit here to Gwen Atkinson who made it so beautifully.

SEARED CHICORY, WILD FLOWER AND HERB SALAD

Wild flowers and herbs: lemon balm , herb robert, cow parsley, parsley, sweet cicely, water mint, red clover.
2 heads chicory cut into quarters or eighths.
2 tbsp oil
Dressing:
1 tbsp elderflower syrup
1 tbsp apple cider vinegar
1 tbsp olive oil
Saute chicory in a pan over a hot flame, in a couple of batches, until browned but not burnt, about 2 minutes. Place on a plate and add the wild herbs and flowers. Pour over the dressing and serve.

SUMMER STIR FRY WITH BITTER GREENS

Stir frying holds the hot and intense energy of the sun, so it's fun for the summer or to bring some of this energy to enliven a meal

Serves 4-6:
1 large carrot, cut into batons
1 red onion cut into strips
1 red pepper cut into strips
10 baby corn halved
1 courgette cut into batons
2 chicory quartered length ways
1/2 broccoli, cut into thin florets
1/2 cup bitter wild summer greens,
dandelion leaves or jack by the hedge
1 tbsp olive oil
Ume vinegar and mirin to season

Saute the onion and carrots in the olive oil, tossing regularly to prevent burning; next, add the pepper and corn, then after a couple of minutes, add the courgette, broccoli and chicory. Then lastly, the wild bitter green leaves. Season to taste.

All these ingredients grow well in an English garden, so it's fun to create such a locally produced salad. Add any additional summer vegetable that you enjoy.

SUMMER VEGETABLE SALAD

Serves 4-5:
4-5 cups summer vegetables:
courgettes, sliced diagonal broad beans, depodded and peeled of outer skin
mange tout, or sugar snap 1-2 tbsp chopped herbs Tahni dressing p.67

Blanch or steam the vegetables until al dente; refresh until cold water. Add the chopped herbs and dressing, and serve.

Strips of vegetables make a nice noodle that's gluten free! This dish is light and you can make it as spicy as fits your mood.

VEGETABLE NOODLES IN COCONUT MILK

Serves 4:
1 tbsp peeled and chopped finely ginger
1-2 cloves garlic, chopped finely
1 tsp cumin and 1/2 tsp turmeric
1 tbsp of coconut oil
2-3 cups coconut milk
1 tbsp shoyu
1 carrot peeled into thin long noodles
1 courgette peeled into thin long noodles
1/2 red pepper cut into thin strips
1 head pak choy or kale cut into strips
12 bay corn quartered length ways
8-10 thin green beans
Fry the ginger, garlic and spices for 5 minutes. Add the coconut milk and shoyu and bring to simmer. Add the carrots, baby corn, green beans and red pepper, cook for 5 minutes then add the courgette and kale, and cook for a further minute or two until all the vegetable strips are soft.

97

Enjoy as a desert or summer breakfast; summer fruits, nuts and oaty crunch is a great combination.

SUMMER BERRY GRANOLA

Serves 4:
For the fruit:
2 cups raspberries or other summer berries
1 tbsp water
Pinch of salt
2 tbsp maple or rice syrup
1 tbsp kuzu, diluted in
For the granola topping:
1 cup pecans or other nuts
1/2 cup sunflower seeds
1 cups oats
1/2 cup maple or rice syrup
2 tbsp coconut oil, heated so it becomes liquid

Place the fruit in a pan with the water and salt; cook on a low heat for 2-3 minutes until the fruit begins to soften and release juices. Add the kuzu and stir for a minute to thicken; add rice syrup to sweeten to your tastes. Place on the bottom of a baking tray with sides. Mix the ingredients for the granola topping together well and spread evenly over the top of the fruit. Bake in an oven pre-heated to 180 degrees C for 20 minutes. Serve, topped with fresh raspberries or other summer fruit.

ROSE AND ELDERFLOWER KANTEN

This is beautifully delicate and fragrant; using the energy of roses and elderflowers to create a desert full of love to open the heart.

Serves 4:
3 cups water
1/2 cup apple concentrate
3 tbsp agar flakes
1 tbsp dried or 40 fresh rose petals
3 heads elderflowers
1/2 tsp salt

Simmer the elderflowers and rose petals in the water for 10 minutes. Remove the flowers; make sure you still have 3 cups water, add more if necessary. Heat the agar in the flower water until dissolved, approx 5-8 mins. Add the salt and juice and stir in; add a few petals as garnish. Cool in the fridge until set.

STRAWBERRY AND VANILLA CAKE

My cakes always have a homemade feel. I have accepted this look now as it has a kind of rustic charm, and plus, they do taste good. This cake is a real treat, it was created during the summer when we were photographing recipes to celebrate Kerttu's birthday. We had a great day; she said the cake tasted of "summer magic and strawberry dreams".

For the cake:
1 cup white and 1 1/2 cup whole spelt flour
1 cup ground almonds
1 tbsp baking powder
1/2 cup olive oil
1/2 cup honey
1/2 cup maple syrup
1/2 cup almond or rice milk
1 tbsp vanilla essence

For the Toppings:
1 carton coconut cream, chilled for 1/2 hour and drained of watery liquid
1 1/2 tbsp maple syrup
1 tsp vanilla
2 tbsp sugar free strawberry jam
3 tbsp water
1 tsp kuzu, diluted in water
1 cup strawberries

Heat oven to 160 degrees C; mix the dry ingredients together. Mix the wet ingredients together, and then mix the wet into the dry. Place in a round 8-9 inch baking mould and bake for 40-45 minutes.

Mix the coconut cream, maple syrup and vanilla together; place in the fridge or freezer to chill for 1/2 hour. Warm the jam and water in a small pan, add the kuzu to thicken, into a glaze.

To Assemble: cover cake with the coconut 'icing', top with strawberries and drizzle over the glaze.

STRAWBERRY FAIRYCAKES

These cakes are really simple to make yet look very effective. Most children love strawberries so don't notice its sugar free sneaky. Not to be dismissed by adults too.

Makes 16 small fairy cakes:
For the cakes:
1 cup wholemeal flour
1 cup plain flour
1 tbsp baking powder
3/4 cup oat milk
1 cup diced strawberries
1/2 cup apple concentrate
1/3 cup olive oil
For the topping:
sugar free strawberry jam,
extra strawberries for the top

Mix all the cake ingredients together, and spoon into fairy cake cases. Cook in the oven pre-heated to 180 degrees C for 15 minutes until golden brown on top. When cooled, put a tsp of jam on top and 2 quarters of strawberries.

RASPBERRY ICE-CREAM

A great dairy and sugar free ice-cream, perfect for cooling on hot summer days. We have no trouble growing raspberries at Sunny Brow, so I have lots of raspberry recipes, this one is really simple and enjoyable. You can use other soft fruits in exchange for the raspberries, such as strawberries or blackberries, I sometimes use lavender too.

Serves 4:
1 cup coconut cream
1 cup raspberries
Pinch of salt
3 tbsp rice syrup

Place the raspberries and salt in a small pan and warm gently until the juices run from the fruit and they become very soft. Remove from heat and allow to cool. Add the rice syrup to taste. Gently stir the raspberries into the coconut cream. Freeze for about 2-3 hours. Serve with summer flowers and mint.

A beautiful desert, light and simple, using the magical elder flowers and summer fruits.

POACHED PEACHES WITH ELDERFLOWER

Serves 4:
4 peaches or nectarines, halved
1 cup water
3-4 elderflower heads
1/2 Vanilla pod, cut length ways
1 tbsp kuzu, diluted in a small
amount of water
1 tbsp rice syrup (optional)

Gently simmer the elderflower and vanilla pod in water for 15 minutes. Add the peach halves, cover and poach until soft, about 5-8 minutes, depending on the size of your peaches. Remove
peaches, peel and lay them on a serving plate. Remove the elderflower heads and place liquid back on low heat. Add the kuzu and warm for 2 minutes to thicken, add the rice syrup to taste; pour the sauce over the peaches and serve, garnished with elderflowers.

Determined to enjoy a elderflower drink that was not made with refined sugar – this is what I came up with.

ELDERFLOWER AND RED BERRY DRINK

---

2 cups water
2 cups apple concentrate
15-20 elderflower heads
1 cup red currants
Juice and zest from 2 lemons

Bring the water to the boil and add the juice and lemons. Turn off heat and add the elderflowers and red currants. Leave for 24 hours. Strain the cordial with a muslin or fine sieve. Mix with some still or sparkling water to
make a refreshing summer drink. Add extra summer fruits into the drink too for a real exotic cocktail feel.

LAVENDER AND WILD ROSE INFUSION

A light and fragrant tea that uses the flowers of the garden to relax and soften our energy. If you fancy this out of season or don't have the fresh flowers, using dried also works really well.

Serves 2-3
2 cups water
40 fresh rose petals or 1 tbsp
dried rose petals
2 lavender heads or 1 level tsp
dried lavender

Infuse the flowers in about 2 cups boling water for 5-10 minutes and serve using a strainer.

LATE SUMMER/
EARLY AUTUMN
AND THE ELEMENT OF EARTH

Lammas, at the beginning of August, seems to mark the beginning of this season. It's a time to celebrate the Earth, the Mother, the Earth our Mother. It's the beginning of a time of great abundance, of receiving the gifts of the Earth, of reaping the rewards of what we have sown and tendered. At Sunny Brow, we gather in celebration of Lammas, making corn dollies, grassy wreaths and plaited corn bread. All over festivals are in abundance, as a time to mark with tribal style gatherings, celebrating life full in richness and love.

We can still have warm sunny days but the intensity of the sun's rays has faded a little, and there is a gentler sensation to its energy. I always feel in this season a sense of coming home . The energy is beginning to ground after the vibrant action of the spring and summer and it can be a time to relax and nurture. The garden and wild vegetation is fruiting and seeding to begin the fertilisation process of the next cycle, and to provide sustenance to take us through the winter months. The colours are beginning to change, warmer grounding yellows and browns start appearing taking us towards the shift of autumn. This phase feels softer than autumn though, it is the gentle coming home with love and nurture that supports and nourishes.

This time of year corresponds to the Earth element, which is about love, mothering, nurture, and receiving and giving. It's a great time to renew after the Fire element has burnt out everything, a good time to stabilise and begin a more grounded phase.

In Season
There is such abundance at this time of year:
corn, apples, plums, pears, blueberries, melons, spinach, runner beans, borlotti beans, shallots, sweetcorn, beetroot, celery, artichokes, gooseberries, kohlrabi, leeks, potatoes, turnips, tomatoes, radishes, endive, carrots, aubergines, cauliflower, kale, pumpkins, butternut squash, salsify, swede, peas, courgettes, summer and other squashes.

In Season, in the wild:
blackberries, bilberries, meadow sweet, yarrow, mugwort, wild peas, currants, raspberries, wild mushrooms, damsons, crab apples, rosehips, elderberries

The Earth element has a feminine energy supporting all living processes and, in essence, is fertility and growth, and of course, a home to all the elements. Everything interacts with the Earth, and it is an integral part of life, forming the rhythm and weaving of it all. Rooted, whole, grounded, and full of abundance and radiant life, those in harmony and at home with themselves are full in Earth energy.

This element is about sweetness, the sweetness in life, flowing through our body, to allow giving and receiving in equal measure, to love oneself and others. In balance, the Earth energy will assist healthy menstruation and fertility, and the ability to nourish oneself and others, it will give us a clear mind and direction. The organs that correspond are stomach and spleen, which energetically govern the functions of nurturing, grounding, bonding, digesting food, and creation and balance of our blood.

Earth is controlled by Tree whose roots put boundaries on Earth's ability to give, so those wanting to tend their Earth energy should make sure the Tree element is not too strong. During counselling sessions, especially with women, I have noticed this can be a common pattern, and definitely one to be aware of. Keeping the "liver and lover" open and light will help to keep Earth happy.

People with an Earth imbalance will love dairy as it is sweet and creamy, a product of Mother. An important point here is not to make the cow your mother. We must step into our own power and not need this energetic support from another animal. If you crave dairy, then concentrate on foods in this section, allowing soft and creamier foods but from plant based sources.

Earth energy is integral to all of life, to nourish and nurture. If this has been imbalanced in our lives, if we did not receive positive mothering, or do not allow ourselves to receive, or perhaps suffer from a lack of connection to Mother Earth, then the Earth energy could become lacking. There can be a manifestation of many things such as weak digestion, tiredness, feeling overwhelmed, anorexia, infertility, instability, unearthed, insecurity, depending too much on others for support, or an unhealthy desperate craving for support from others and a lack of imagination and sympathy.

Here we must take care by eating warming, centring, creamy and softening foods. Add homeliness to your life, allowing nurture from massage, or connection with friends, your mother or other women who can hold this energy. Choose sweet, round, on the ground veggies that grow on the Earth, squashes, sweet potato and pumpkins, and vegetables that overlap themselves, such as onions, cabbage, artichokes. Choose round, tightly packed foods, like the Earth, millet, chickpeas, hazelnuts, apples and pears. Choose longer cooking methods, that bring out the sweetness of these foods, avoid cold foods as these can weaken the Earth organs.

If there is too much Earth, there can be a strong contractive energy. The body can tighten, especially the stomach and solar plexus area, symptoms can be acid reflux, bloating, obesity, nausea, sinus congestion,
worry, obsessive thoughts, over eating, gathering of clutter, over thinking, disconnection to own feelings, troubles and cramps related to menstrual flow, sleep disturbance, weight fluctuation, and not caring for oneself.

109

To help this imbalance, begin to reduce Earth energy by avoiding too much of Earth's sweetness or any heavy foods; include Fire and opening Tree foods, lots of green vegetables and light opening foods, and softer, gentle foods such as soups and blanched vegetable salads. To help the energy, clear up clutter in the home, find space to rest and nurture yourself, and get out in nature for gentle, expansive walks to open the mind and body.

General guidelines for any Earth imbalance are to balance work and rest, find regularity, avoid overindulgence, especially with food, walk bare foot in nature, receive a massage, cook a meal for yourself, meditate in nature, avoid dairy and replace with wholesome nurturing foods with a soft opening energy, such as soups, on the ground vegetables, salads, and warm cooked foods. Find ways of enjoying sweetness in your life in a balanced way, such as soft cooked vegetables, alternative sweeteners and fruits, and time with loving family or friends.

EARTH ENERGY AND EATING; FINDING BALANCE

Earth and eating are so very entwined; the Earth provides the food we eat, how we consume it is important for over all health of body and mind, and a healthy connection to Earth. An obvious sign that Earth energy is out of balance is negative eating patterns, such as eating in a hurry, skipping meals, not cooking for oneself, controlled eating, and also the more serious conditions, such as anorexia and buleima, that are becoming an increased problem in our society.

By studying and bringing this element into balance, we can support ourselves to combat poor eating habits. However, if we have low self esteem and a negative relationship to our body, an emotional imbalance that can occur from damaged Earth energy, it is hard to want to nourish or care for the body, to love yourself and honour it with good food, and therefore, the problem is exacerbated and a vicious circle is formed.

Take steps to build a more positive self-image and put good things in your body by following the recipes and recommendations to balance the Earth element in this section. However, do try to avoid becoming too strict with yourself, invite in the good rather than banish the 'bad' to bring a calm balance to the body. Finding a good relationship to your Earth energy will include increasing self esteem, self worth and love for yourself.

Good guidelines for optimum support around eating are: eat regular meals, Earth likes moderation and regularity; avoid random and careless eating; eat calmly, with reverence to the food and the Earth from which it came; chew well; eat sitting down; don't eat too late, or within three hours of bedtime; consume beverages at room temperature or warmer.

It is hard to conquer some of these things once the Earth energy is out of balance, but trying to bring in healthy eating practices, as well as working on yourself holistically, will gradually bring about more balance. If you are concerned about your eating habits, or feel you may need more support in this area, I recommend seeing macrobiotic councellor, or someone similar, who can offer support, emotionally and physically whilst making a change.

BEETROOT SOUP

Beetroots make a great soup as they are a hearty, sweet and tasty vegetable. This is a fantastic Earth energy dish. Beetroots are nourishing for the female reproductive system, especailly the womb, and interestingly, beetroots 'bleed' their juice into the water as you cook them.

Serves 4:
4 small to medium beetroots, cubed
1 large onion, diced
2 cloves of garlic, chopped finely
1 tsp salt
1 bay leaf
4 cups water or vegetable stock

Saute beetroot, onions and garlic for 10 minutes, with the salt. Add the stock and bay leaf. Bring to the boil, cover and cook for 30-40 minutes until the beetroot is soft. Remove the bay leaf and blend until smooth. Serve with toasted pumpkin seeds on the top. Or also nice with tofu sour cream p.67.

SWEETCORN CHOWDER

I get excited when the sweetcorn arrives in the veg box and markets in its jacket. Tinned or frozen can work in this recipe too but it's no way near as good. Seasonal sweetcorn is tender and delicious, and also good value to buy. The addition of squash to a chowder gives it an even sweeter taste and a lovely relaxing energy, perfect for this time of year.

Serves 4:
4 large corn on the cobs, or 3-4 tins
1/2 large butternut squash, cut into small
1 cm cubes
1 onion, diced
1/2 tsp salt
2 tbsp oil
1/2 cup polenta
1-2 tbsp sweet miso
6 cups water

If you have fresh corn, shear the corn off the cob and place the cobs in the 6 cups water; bring to the boil, cover, turn down and simmer for 20 minutes. Prepare the vegetables, and then sauté the onion in the oil with the salt for 5-10 minutes. Add the squash and corn and then after 5 more minutes of sauteeing, add the polenta and water from the cobs. Bring to the boil and simmer for 20 minutes. Check and add enough water to make a desired consistency, and partly blend the soup. Season to taste with the sweet miso, and serve, topped with steamed greens and toasted seeds.

Really tasty and enjoyable for all the family, these sweetcorn cakes are a delicious savoury dish. Using gram flour makes them hearty and nutritious, full of protein and good for balancing blood sugars. I like to take them on picnics and serve them with tofu sour cream for a simple lunch or tea.

SWEETCORN PATTIES

Makes 20 Patties:
2 tins sweetcorn
1 medium onion, diced small
1 clove garlic, diced finely
1 tsp salt
1 tbsp olive oil
1 cup gram flour
1 tsp cumin

Saute the onions, cumin, garlic and salt in the oil for 10 minutes until the onions are soft and sweet. Add the sweetcorn and partially blend using a hand blender. Mix in the flour to form a thick batter. Heat 2-3 tsp oil in a pan and fry 4-5 patties on a medium heat (1 heaped tbsp batter per patty), turning to cook both sides and prevent burning. Cook until the patties are firm and golden on both sides.

MILLET AND SQUASH "RISOTTO"

Creamy and satisfying, this dish is a super dish for this time of year and also very supportive for feminine energy. Millet gets really creamy and adding the salty miso makes this dish a great vegan substitute for cheesy dishes.

1 cup millet
3 cups water/stock
1/2 butternut squash or pumpkin, cut into
1 cm cubes (about 3 cups when cubed)
1 onion, diced
1 tbsp olive oil
1/2 tsp salt
1 tbsp bouillon
1 tbsp sweet miso
1 tbsp ume vinegar
1 tbsp herbs to garnish

Toast the millet in a hot dry pan until nutty and golden. Sauté the onion and squash with the salt in the olive oil for about 10 minutes. Add the millet, bouillion and water, and bring to the boil. Turn down to very low, use a flame spreader if you have one, and cook for 20 minutes. Stir in the sweet miso and ume vinegar, and garnish with some parsley or coriander to serve.

CHICKPEA AND BUTTERNUT CURRY

A mild aromatic curry with sweet vegetables and wholesome chickpeas. A really yummy dish for late summer evenings. Serve with rice or millet and some steamed or sautéed green vegetables for a beautifully balanced and nutritious meal.

1 medium butternut squash, cubed
1 large onion, diced
2 cups cooked or tins chickpeas (or home cooked better if poss)
2 cloves garlic, finely chopped
2" piece ginger, finely chopped
1/2 tsp dried chilli flakes (optional)
1 tsp cumin
1/2 tsp turmeric
1 tsp mixed spice
1 tin tomatoes (optional)
Handful of kale leaves, stem removed and thinly sliced
1 tbsp fresh coriander, chopped

Sauté onion for 5 minutes with 1 tsp salt. Add ginger, garlic and spices and sauté for 5 minutes more. Add squash and tomatoes. Cover with water to just at level of vegetables. Cook for approx 20 minutes or until all veg is soft. Add kale and chickpeas and cook for a further 5 minutes. Add some oat cream and garnish with, or stir in, the coriander.

Using chickpea flour adds depth and texture to this lovely savoury pancake, also a good one for gluten free people. Adding sweet vegetables fills the pancake with nourishment for the Earth energy.

GRAM PANCAKES AND SWEET VEGETABLES

For the pancakes, makes 12-14:
2 cups gram flour
1 cup buckwheat flour
2 tbsp olive oil
1 1/2 cup rice or oat milk
2 cups water
For the sweet vegetable filling:
1/2 squash, cubed
1 sweet potato, cubed
1 2" piece kombu
1 tbsp sweet miso
For the onion relish:
1 large red onion, diced
1/2 salt
1/2 tsp ground coriander
2 tbsp fresh coriander

Mix the ingredients for the pancakes and leave to stand, in the fridge, whilst preparing the fillings. Place the kombu in the bottom of a pan, vegetables on top and an inch of water. Cover and cook for 15-20 minutes until the vegetables are very soft and the water has evaporated. Remove the kombu and mash with the sweet miso. Saute the onion with the salt and coriander, in 1 tbsp oil, on a very low heat, for about 20 minutes, until the onions are soft and sweet. Add the fresh coriander. Coat a pan with oil and fry the pancakes for 1 minute on each side. To serve, fill with the vegetables and onion relish.

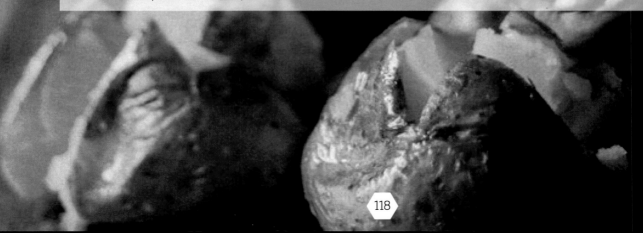

Potatoes are in season in late summer and autumn, they don't feature in a classic macrobiotic diet but I really love their energy and use them moderately. They are lighter than the other vegetables that grow in the ground and baked, they are delicious. In my opinion, this recipe gives the nicest baked pots. Serve with hummus or a borlotti bean puree and salad for a tasty and seasonal late summer supper.

ROASTED SPUDS WITH BOLOTTI BEAN PUREE

Sreves 4-6:
4-6 medium potatoes
1 tbsp olive oil
1 level tsp salt
For the bolotti hummus:
Copy hummus recipe but using bolotti beans instead of chickpeas.

Rub the potatoes with the oil and salt. Place in an oven preheated to 180 degrees C and cook for approximately 1 hour. Blend all the ingredients together for the bean puree. Open the cooked potatoes and drizzle in olive oil. Serve with the puree and a tasty salad.

HUMMUS WITH SWEET POTATO WEDGES

A delicious party dish, light lunch, but also use these recipes separately to add yummy Earth energy to any other lunch or dinner. The hummus is amazingly easy to make. Both these dishes are a great addition to family foods, as they are enjoyed by kids and adults.

4-5 sweet potatoes, cut length ways into wedges.
2 tbsp olive oil
For the Hummus:
1 1/2 cups of softly cooked chickpeas or 1 tin chickpeas
Juice of 1/2 lemon
1/4 cup olive oil
1 clove garlic, chopped finely
1 tsp tahini
1 tsp ume paste
1 tsp sweet miso

Bring a pan of water to the boil. Add the sweet potato and blanch for 5 minutes. Place in an oven tray with the olive oil and cook in oven preheated to 200 degrees C for 30-40 minutes until crispy and sweet. Toss during cooking to prevent burning. Blend all the ingredients together for the hummus and garnish with extra chickpeas and paprika.

Chickpeas are round like the Earth and will nourish this element. This is a really quick and simple dish once you have some cooked chickpeas, see p40 for instructions, alternatively, for a super quick meal, you can use tinned.

CHICKPEAS WITH SWEET MISO

Serves 4-6
1 1/2 cups cooked chickpeas, or 1 tin
2 carrots, cut in diagonal half moons
1 large leek, sliced thin on a diagonal
1-2 tbsp sweet miso
1 tbsp kuzu or arrowroot, diluted in a little water.
1 tbsp fresh coriander, chopped

Sauté the leeks and the carrots in a little oil for 5 minutes. Add a cup of water and the chickpeas, and cook until the vegetables are soft. Add arrowroot or kuzu to thicken and finally, add the herbs and the miso, and serve warm.

QUINOA SALAD

This is a scrummy and interesting salad; served with a nice soup, it makes a balanced lunch or supper. I very often serve this, or variations like it, at my retreats and workshops, as it is easy to make and suits group cooking. Quinoa is a great addition to the diet, protein rich, nutritious and gluten free.

Serves 4-6
1 cup quinoa
2 cups water
1/2 cup cubed squash
1/2 cup sunflower and/or pumpkin seeds
1/2 red onion/2 spring onions, diced small
2 tbps fresh chopped herbs, coriander, mint and/or parsley
Dressing:
1 tbsp ume vinegar
1 tbsp rice vinegar
1 tsp mustard
Grated rind of one lemon
1 tbsp olive oil

Rub the cubed squash in olive oil and bake in a preheated oven for 20 minutes until soft.
Toast the quinoa in a pan until it smells nutty, be careful not to burn. Add the water, make sure you don't add more than 2 cups of water as this salad suits the quinoa to be more al dente than over cooked. Bring it to the boil, cover and simmer for 20-25 minutes. All the water will have gone. Cool quickly, I normally place it in a stainless steel bowl in cold water. Toast the seeds. When everything has cooled, mix all the ingredients together and serve.

A great salad for late summer using blanched cabbage, crunchy apples, nuts and sea vegetables. A dish loaded with essential vitamins and minerals.

APPLE, ARAME AND BLANCHED CABBAGE SALAD

---

1 apple, grated or cut into thin batons
1/2 white cabbage
1/2 cup arame, soaked for 15 minutes
1/2 cup walnuts, toasted and chopped
tahini dressing from p 67

Blanch the cabbage in a pan of boiling water for 2 minutes, refresh under cold water.
Mix all the ingredients together and serve with the tahini dressing.

PUMPKIN AND COCONUT SOUP

I love the combination of squashes and or root vegetables with coconut milk. The combination gives a warming satisfying soup with the creamy lightness of coconut milk giving an interesting twist.

Serves 4-6:
1 medium culinary pumpkin or large butternut squash, peeled and chopped into chunks
1 large onion, chopped into chunks
1 tsp ground cumin
1 cup coconut milk
1-2 tbsp sweet miso

Saute the onion and pumpkin with the cumin, and a little salt to bring out the sweetness, for 5-10 minutes. Add 5 cups water and bring to simmer. Cook for 20 minutes or until all the vegetables are soft. Add coconut milk and bring back to temperature. Remove from heat and add miso. Blend until smooth and serve topped with toasted pumpkin seeds.

SWEET VEGETABLE DRINK

Made with sweet vegetables, this is a healing drink for Earth energy to balance blood sugars and to receive a sweetness that is healthy and pure. It is relaxing and nutritious. You can use whichever sweet vegetables you have in the cupboard, there isn't really a set recipe, but the guidelines below will help you create this healing drink.

Serves 1-2:
2 cups sweet vegetables chopped
Choose from:
carrots, parsnips, butternut squash,
swede, sweet potatoes
6 cups water

Bring all the vegetables to simmer in the water. Simmer for 10-15 minutes. Strain and serve

Inspired by a lovely Spanish helper, Gillum, this dish uses the pizza base from p.78 and some slowly cooked sweet onions, which is actually a great Earth dish and can also be used without the pizza base as an onion butter.

CARAMELISED ONION TART

Serves 6-8
6 large onions, cut into half moons
2 tbsp oil
1 tsp salt
1/2 quantity of pizza dough, p82
1 egg (optional)

Begin to fry the onions with the oil and salt. Once hot, turn them to a very low heat to cook slowly for about 45 minutes-1 hour. Stir occasionally to make sure they don't burn. Preheat an oven to 200 degrees C. Make the dough and roll out to fit a medium sized baking tray. Lay the onions on top and cook in the oven for 10-15 minutes. You can also whisk and spread one egg over the top before cooking to a cheesy texture.

Any sweet vegetable will make a great sweet puree, combine with oil and cook slowly and you can achieve a great buttery richness that is an enjoyable addition to a meal or as a snack on wholemeal bread or crackers. Carrots and onions work well like this, but here is a beetroot butter.

BEETROOT BUTTER

4 beetroots, grated
1 large red onion, cut into thin half moons
1 heaped tsp salt
2 tbsp olive oil
1 cup water

Saute the vegetables with the oil and salt for 10 minutes. Add the water and cook very slowly on a very low heat for 2 hours. Stir occasionally to prevent sticking and burning. Blend or purre and serve warm or cold.

A dish inspired from using the vegetables after making a sweet vegetable drink, as I hate waste. However, this does compromise the taste a little, as some of the flavour has gone into the drink. Cook fresh for best results, but don't rule out making the most of leftovers.

SWEET VEG MASH

Cube 3-4 cups of on-the-ground and root vegetables; choose from:
swede
butternut squash
carrot
parsnip
celeriac

Saute for 5 minutes with a pinch of salt. Add a piece of kombu to the bottom of the pan and an inch of two of water. Cook until all the vegetables are soft, about 15 minutes, and all the water has evaporated. Top up with a little water whilst cooking if needed.

Soft and satisfying, this is a lovely side dish to compliment any meal.

NISHIME

2 carrots
2 onions
1/2 squash
1/2 swede
1 piece kombu
1 tbsp shoyu or
sweet miso

Add the chunks of vegetables to a pan, with the kombu at the bottom, and add 1 inch water. Cover with a lid and bring to the boil. Simmer until all the vegetables are soft and all the water has evaporated. Make sure it doesn't go dry and burn, and also if you have too much water, once cooked, you can boil water off quickly. Season to taste and serve.

This combination of vegetables works so well together. A lovely salad for days when you feel overwhelmed and craving expansion. Liven up your meal with this dish, that is energetic but grounding too.

BEETROOT AND RED
CABBAGE SALAD

1 small red onion, cut in thin half moons
2 beetroot, grated
1/2 red cabbage, sliced finely
2 tsp salt
1 tsp fennel seeds

Add all the ingredients to a bowl, and massage the salt into the vegetables for about 5 minutes, beginning to soften them and release their water. Place in a salad press or use a plate and weight on top to add pressure. Press for at least an hour. Serve with a nice dressing p.66

Nicknamed 'the queen of the meadow', meadowsweet has a fantastic energy, elegant light and regal. This desert is lovely, served warm or chilled. It's also easy to dry the flower heads to enjoy their energy later in the year, simply hang in bunches of 4-5, not too compacted to dry.

MEADOWSWEET AND PECAN DESSERT

Serves 4
1 1/2 cup rice or almond milk
1/2 cup amazake
1/2 cup pecans, toasted and ground
3 heads meadowsweet, fresh or dried
2 tbsp kuzu, diluted in a little rice milk

Simmer the meadowsweet flowers in the milk for about 5 minutes. Strain and then add the amazake and pecans to the milk, warm through, then stir in the kuzu to thicken. Serve warm or chilled, sprinkled with some toasted, chopped pecans on top.

A nice twist to a classic cake; beetroot adds nutrition sweetness and depth to the chocolate experience. This is also a good gluten free cake recipe. Add raisins, chopped nuts and/or sugar free chocolate chips for interesting variations.

CHOCOLATE AND BEETROOT BROWNIE

2 small beetroot, grated
4 tbsp oil
1 tsp salt
2 cups ground almond
1 cup gram flour
1/2 cup buckwheat flour
1 cup cocoa powder
1/2 cup rice syrup
1/2 cup maple syrup or honey
1 cup almond milk

Saute the beetroot in the olive oil with the salt for 20 minutes, make sure the heat is low so it cooks slowly to bring out the sweetness. Mix the dry ingredients together. Mix the wet ingredients, adding the cooked beetroot, and add to the dry ingredients. Line a brownie tin and pour in the mixture. Cook in an oven preheated to 160 degrees C for 25-30 minutes.

BLACKBERRY AND APPLE SPREAD

A great way to use and preserve foraged blackberries, and to continue their adventurous energy throughout autumn. This is a sugar free fruit spread that uses apple concentrate instead of white sugar to sweeten. It does not keep as well as jam but will keep if freshly sealed after making, for a few weeks in the fridge .

5 cups blackberries
6 cups water
1/2 tsp salt
Approximately 2 cups apple concentrate
2 tbsp agar flakes

Place the berries and water in a preserve pan or large saucepan. Bring to the boil, turn down to very low and cook for 1-2 hours, or until you have approximately 2 cups of liquid.

Strain the liquid from the pips, I like to do this as wild brambles have large pips. Return the liquid to the pan, add the salt and agar flakes and simmer gently until the agar has dissolved, about 5 minutes. Add the apple concentrate to taste, you may need more or less depending on your own taste and the sweetness of your blackberries. Pour into sterilised glass jars, and store in the fridge.

FRUIT CRUMBLE

You can't beat a crumble. This is a vegan and sugar free crumble that gets much praise. Use any local early autumn fruit you can harvest, forage or buy for good value in the shops.

Serves 6-8:
6-8 pieces of fruit which gives about 4 cups when cut into cubes; choose from:
Pears, peeled
Apples, peeled
Plums or damsons
Blackberries
1-2 tbsp rice or fruit syrup
1 tbsp kuzu
For the crumble:
2 cups rolled oats
1 cup flour
1/2 cup rice syrup
1/4 cup barley malt syrup
3 tbsp oil

Cook the fruit in a pan, together with a splash of water to prevent burning. Add a pinch of salt to encourage the water from the fruit. Cover, turn the heat to low and cook fruit in the juices for about 10 minutes or until all the fruit is soft. Add the kuzu and stir well until thickened. Add the sweetener to taste, the amount you use will depend on how tart your fruit. Place the cooked fruit in the bottom of a glass or ceramic baking dish. Mix the crumble ingredients together and spread evenly on top of the fruit. Bake in an oven preheated at 180 degrees C for 20 minutes or until the crumble is golden on top.

Elegantly simple, this is a fantastic fruit desert that is creamy and delicious, and takes minutes to prepare.

APPLE AND HAZELNUT MOUSSE

Serves 4:
4 large sweet apples
3/4 cup apple juice
1 large tbsp almond or hazlenut butter
Pinch of salt
1 tbsp kuzu diluted with a little water
1-2 tbsp rice syrup (optional)

Peel and cut the apples into cubes, place in a pan with the juice and salt. Simmer until the apples are soft and mash until smooth. Add the nut butter and kuzu and stir to thicken. Add rice syrup to taste. Serve in little glass jars and expect wows of delight.

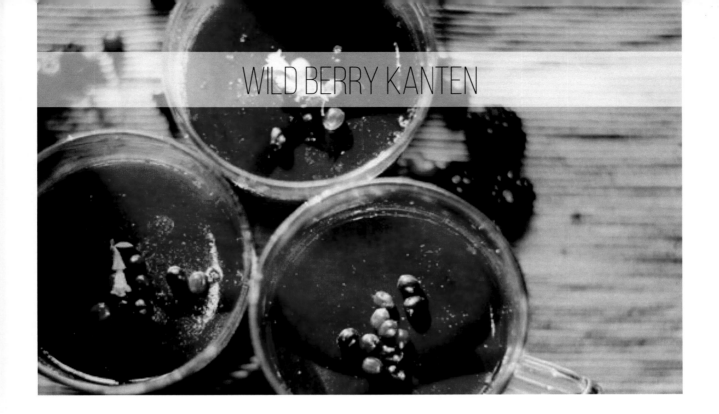

WILD BERRY KANTEN

Harnessing the adventurous energy of blackberry and the heart opening properties of hawthorn, this wild kanten is great fun to forage and cook. It's super nutritious too, as they contain heaps of vitamin C.

Serves 4-6:
2 cups blackberry
1/2 cup hawthorn berries
4 cups water
Approx. 3 tbsp agar flakes
1 tbsp tahini
Pinch of salt
1/2 cup apple concentrate or rice syrup
sweetener to taste

Simmer the blackberries and other berries in the water for 20-30 minutes on a low heat. Strain, removing the seeds. Check how much liquid you have in cup measure and add 1 tbsp agar for each cup of liquid. Simmer with the agar until it dissolves. Add a pinch of salt, rice syrup to taste and whisk in tahini. Put in the fridge until set.

MEADOWSWEET INFUSION

The 'queen of the hedgerow' in a tea gives a beautiful and delicate tea, nourishing for the stomach and digestive system. Meadow sweet is also an anti inflammatory so a great healing herb for many ailments.

Serves 3-4:
2 heads meadow sweet flowers
3 cups water

In a tea pot, add the meadow sweet and boiling water. Steep for at least 5 minutes and serve.

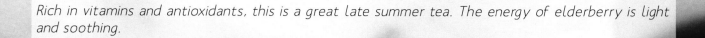

Rich in vitamins and antioxidants, this is a great late summer tea. The energy of elderberry is light and soothing.

BLACKBERRY INFUSION

Serves 2-3:
2 cups blackberries
2 tbsp hawthorn berries
3 cups water
Place the berries in a pan and bring to the boil. Simmer for 15 minutes to allow the berries to release their flavour. Strain and serve.

AUTUMN

AND THE ELEMENT OF METAL

The world is changing, the days are getting shorter as the nights draw in; colours are dramatically changing now from greens through to browns and oranges, and many trees and plants are releasing their leaves. There is a strong energy of letting go and movement to the darker months.

It's another great season, the changes are so significant that it's impossible not to feel the shifts. Although I often feel a grief of the letting go of the vibrancy of the previous seasons, to honour this shift, to feel the grief and then allow it to wash, though, helps me to stay more present and free.

Whenever there is a time of shift, there is an opportunity for transformation. In nature, life force is being taken from the leaves and the outward expression of the trees, and down into the roots. The trees will store only the goodness, releasing anything they don't need as the leaves fall. As the leaves change colour and fall, we, too, can purify and release, using this shift to release anything that no longer serves us, anything that may have built up that we would rather let go of. Also don't be frightened to let go of positive things, life is a cycle of shift and change, nothing can stay the same. Autumn is the time to start turning inwards, to rest more; the unseen world comes closer, I feel mystery and embracing the dark, the veils between the worlds are thin and it is a great time to connect and honour our ancestors.

The colder days make us wrap up warmer and the foods we choose become warmer and more grounding to help in this journey. Mother Earth provides the vegetables that grow deep into the ground, parsnips, carrots, garlic, ginger, vegetables in abundance, especially root vegetables, yet with some opening and mineral rich greens and kales. I begin to bake more in this season. The oven becomes a closer friend again after the lighter foods and cooking styles of spring and summer. We can use more oil and nuts in our cuisine, as their high fat content nourishes and protects us from the cold by creating more heat in the body. The food growing has a stronger energy, to help with cold, to help support in a time of change. Kale is a particularly great food here, it is high in minerals and vitamins to give strength as we head towards winter.

In season
celeriac,cauliflower, kale, leeks, parsnips, pears,
spinach, potatoes, sqaushes, turnips, swedes,
winter radishes, jerusalem artichokes, mooli,
nuts and seeds, carrots, kale, calvo nero,
swede, leeks

In season in the wild
dandelion root, rosehips, acorns, beech nuts, wild
mushrooms, hazelnuts, nettle seeds, sweet chest-
nut, walnuts.

138

This is the season of the Metal energy; letting go, order, organisation, strong boundaries, discernment, separation, the colour white; the related organs are lungs and large intestines. Understanding the Metal element from nature, we see it gives us strength and minerals, beauty from jewels, and long lasting endurance. This is a strong, more masculine energy with beauty too, an indestructible purity, a reinforcement, but it is also one of loss and release, weapons made of metals can cut through and kill; a sword can cut through to truth and clarity. Just as the energy of plants goes deep inside, so the energy of animals and our own bodies goes deep inside, creating more inner warmth and strength. This strength helps us to keep warm as it gets colder and helps to keep infections out.

The emotion is grief and the act of letting go. These emotions are commonly ignored in our culture, particularly by the stereotype of how a man should behave. However, to stop the feeling of grief, or to push it away, can damage our Metal element. If we embrace our grief and allow it to move through us, it enhances our strength, rather than weaken us; to grieve makes us human to remind us that we can love and fully embrace life. If we allow the release that grief gifts us, we can move on in freedom. The strength of Metal can hold us as we let go, as we prepare for, and begin, the journey of release into the winter, into dark, hibination and death.

It has always been a challenge for me to understand this element as it seemed like a strange duality, the strong Metal with release and letting go. I now understand that they are intrinsically linked and it is not weak to let go; in fact, it takes strength to let go, which then in turn allows us to continue to stay strong.

So what happens when Metal is lacking? We will have less strength and less ability to let go. Symptoms can be shortness of breath, fatigue, easily picking up infections like colds and flu, pale/white skin, weak cough, asthma, weak voice, constipation, IBS, exhaustion, inability to grieve, and to complete projects (as this is a letting go), always late, and a tendency to be scattered.

For these conditions, from a lack of Metal, it is good to use the Metal foods: white vegetables, daikon, turnips, horseradish, dark green lentils, all whole grains, but especially short grain brown rice, and all the root vegetables which will give strength and internal energy. Sometimes cook using a pressure cooker and an oven for their strong dynamic energy. Fire melts Metal, so if you are lacking Metal, be careful of the Fire foods, such as fruits and fruit juices, raw salads, and spices.

When the Metal is too strong, too much energy goes deep in the body, which can become hard and stiff and create hard and inflexible thinking and emotions. There will be more energy of the processes than is needed in the body. Symptoms can be acne, hives, pain and cramping, neurotic behaviour, OCD, being overly judgmental, persistent grief, psoriasis , rigid perfectionism, obsessive about punctuality, a strong need to be in control, always on time/early, harsh boundaries, cold, unloving, distant, isolation from people and love.

When the Metal is too strong, then eat the pungent tastes that can disperse the overly contracted energy in the body, stimulating and preventing stagnation. These are garlic, onions, chilli, horseradish, fennel, dill, mustard greens, cinnamon, spring onions, ginger, black pepper. Also eat the Tree and Fire foods that will help the energy release and melt the Metal. Avoid dry foods, baked foods, hard baked bread, cracker and pastry, and reduce excessive meat, chicken, cheese and eggs in the diet.

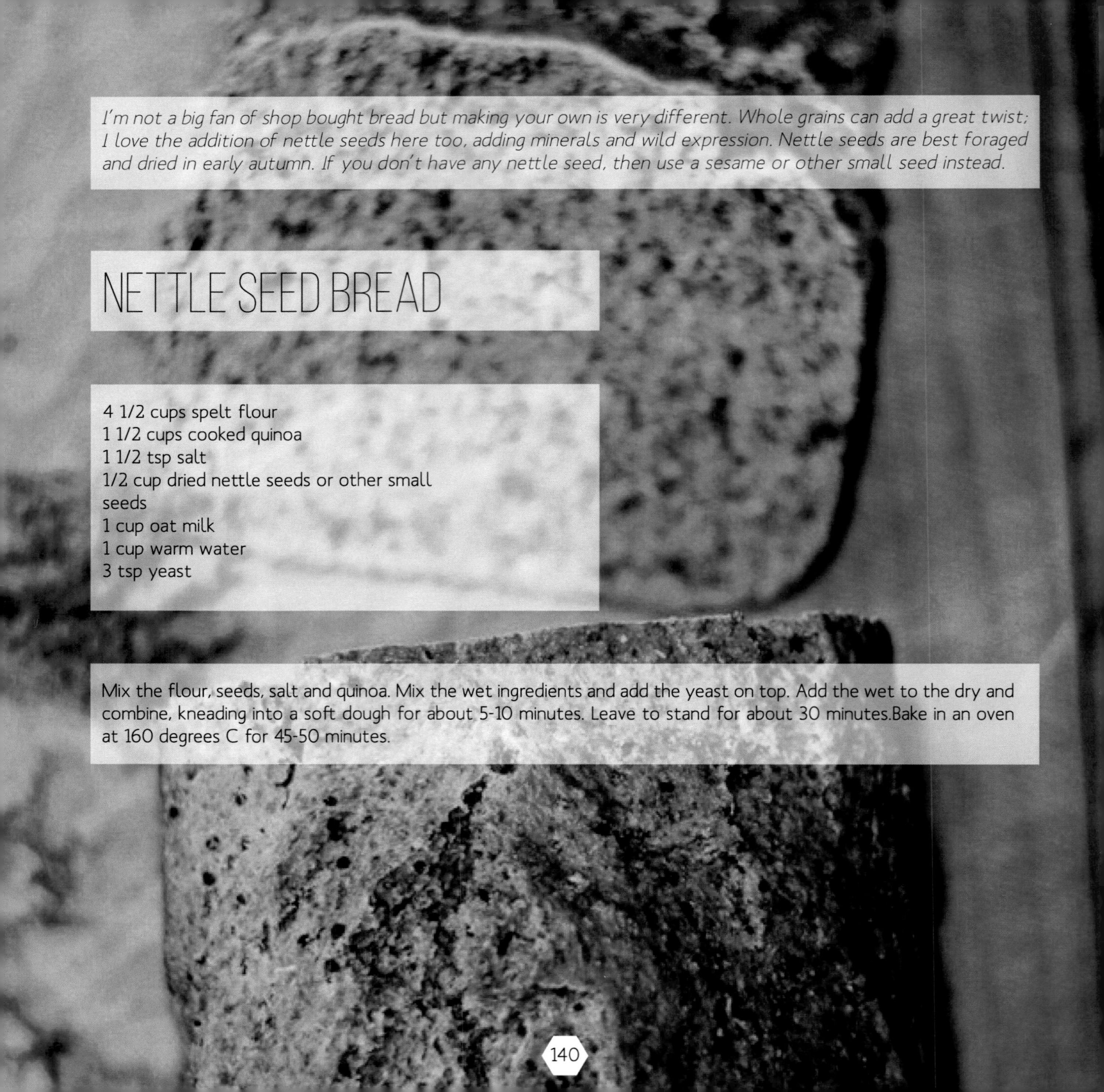

I'm not a big fan of shop bought bread but making your own is very different. Whole grains can add a great twist; I love the addition of nettle seeds here too, adding minerals and wild expression. Nettle seeds are best foraged and dried in early autumn. If you don't have any nettle seed, then use a sesame or other small seed instead.

NETTLE SEED BREAD

4 1/2 cups spelt flour
1 1/2 cups cooked quinoa
1 1/2 tsp salt
1/2 cup dried nettle seeds or other small
seeds
1 cup oat milk
1 cup warm water
3 tsp yeast

Mix the flour, seeds, salt and quinoa. Mix the wet ingredients and add the yeast on top. Add the wet to the dry and combine, kneading into a soft dough for about 5-10 minutes. Leave to stand for about 30 minutes.Bake in an oven at 160 degrees C for 45-50 minutes.

WILD MUSHROOM SOUP

The essence of autumn, wild mushrooms are exciting to find and can be really tasty to eat. They are high in protein and have an earthy connective energy. Make sure you 100% know which are edible before you, put them in a soup. I am lucky enough to have a good friend who is a mushroom expert, and runs courses from Sunny Brow each autumn. He gives me lovely, large hen of the woods which I use for this soup. Thanks Andrew Tomlinsin for the mushrooms and your mushroom knowledge. This soup uses hen of the woods and also chanterelles, as these are quite common at Sunny Brow, but actually you can use any edibles you find, hedgehog mushrooms and porcinis also work well.

4 cups wild mushrooms, chopped
1 tbsp oil
1 onion, diced
1 tsp salt
1-2 cloves garlic, finely chopped
1 potato or 1/2 cup borlotti beans
4 cups water with 1 tbsp bouillon
1 tsp mixed herbs
1/2 cup oat cream

Saute the onion with the oil and salt for 5 minutes. Add the garlic and herbs and continue sauting for a couple more minutes. Add the mushrooms. Chop, and add the potatoes, or add the beans, add water and boullion. Bring to boil, turn to low heat and simmer for 20 minutes. Add the cream and blend to a smooth soup. Serve garnished with chopped herbs and or pickles.

PUY LENTIL STEW WITH DUMPLINGS

This is a warming stew that is nourishing as the weather starts to turn and the nights draw in. I enjoy feeding this to the children (who love it!) as I know is full of vitamins and minerals to balance their bodies and digestive systems.

Serves 6;
1 large onion, diced
2 medium to large carrots, diced
2 sticks celery, diced
2 cups puy lentils
7 cups water
1 tbsp bouillon
2 tsp mixed herbs
2 cloves garlic, chopped finely
2 tbsp shoyu
1 tbsp apple concentrate
1 tbsp parsley, chopped fine
For the Dumplings:
2 cups wholemeal spelt flour
1 cup vegetable suet
3/4 cup warm water

Mix the dumpling mixture together and cover whilst beginning the stew. In a large pan, saute the onion, carrots and celery with a pinch of salt for 5 minutes. Add the garlic and herbs and saute for a couple more minutes. Add the lentils, stir them in, and then add the stock. Form the dumplings into golf ball size rounds, and add to the top of the stew under the stock. Once boiling, simmer for approx 30-45 minutes until you have a thick stew with soft dumplings. Don't stir the stew until about half way through cooking as the dumplings are too delicate. Add the shoyu and apple concentrate towards the end of cooking. Add the parsley and stir in, or leave on top as garnish, and serve.

I love autumn, and this pie embodies all I love; it is my own version of a dish from 'Gillam's', a great cafe in Ulverston. The Earth element vegetables, round and on the ground, can also support us in the late autumn; they are in season and therefore good value. Combining them with some homegrown potatoes and autumnal herbs, and baking in the oven makes for great late autumn magic.

SAVOURY PUMPKIN PIE

1 medium butternut squash or pumpkin,
peeled and cubed in 1-2cm chunks
1 large onion, cut into 1cm half moons
2 tbsp olive oil
2-3 potatoes, cubed in 1-2cm chunks
1-2 cloves garlic, finely chopped
4-5 sage leaves, finely sliced
1 tbsp mirin, 1 tbsp shoyu
For the pastry base:
3 cups flour
4 tbsp oil
3/4 cup water
1/2 tsp salt

Heat the over to 180 degrees C. Saute the squash and onion in the olive oil with a tsp of salt. Cook for about 10 minutes. Add the garlic and sage and cook for another 5 minutes. Add the potatoes and an inch of water, cover and cook the vegetables for about 15-20 minutes until they are soft and all the water has gone. Add mirin and shoyu 5 minutes from the end of cooking. For pastry: rub the oil into the flour. Add water and combine. Avoid overworking the dough. Roll out on a cold surface with a little flour, if needed, to prevent sticking. Rub a little oil on the bottom of a flan or pie dish and lay in the pastry base; top with the squash mixture; bake for 25 minutes.

1 - Prepare the vegetables to go inside the sushi, by cutting them into long thin strips.

2 - Spread the tahini or peanut butter and ume paste across the middle of the rice. Lay your chosen vegetable strips on top in the middle.

3 - Place the nori on the sushi mat, rough side up with the strips running away from you. With damp hands, push 1/2 cup rice onto a nori sheet in a rectangle about 4" high from the base.

4 - Roll the nori, tucking it into the rice. Keep a firm pressure as you roll. As you get to the last inch of nori, place a lttle water on the edge and complete the roll. Push gently to bond the nori.

5 - Using a sharp knife, cut the sushi into even pieces and place on a serving plate with some soy sauce dip.

6 - Gather the ingredients to make the sushi. Include a small cup of water.

STEP BY STEP: VEGETARIAN SUSHI

Sushi has the energy of Metal. Strong, neat and organised. It makes for a delicious lunch, snack or enjoy as part of a full meal. It's really easy to make once you know the technique. Follow these steps for simple great tasting sushi.

Makes 4 rolls:
3-4 cups of cooked short or medium
grain brown rice
2 tbsp sauerkraut
1/2 carrot
3" piece cucumber
2 spring onions
2 tbsp peanut butter or 1 tbsp tahini
2 tsp ume paste
4 sheets nori

A flat pizza like bread with pumpkin chunks on top that are pre-baked in the oven first. This was first cooked for me by an Italian guy and I ran with it to suit our ingredients here. It's great to strengthen the Metal energy, as it's hearty from baking.

PUMPKIN FLAT BREAD

For the bread:
1 culinary pumpkin, cut into 1cm cubes
1 tbsp finely chopped sage
1-2 cloves garlic, chopped finely
1 tsp salt
2 tbsp olive oil

For the bread:
3 cups flour (1 white and 2 wholemeal)
2 tbsp oil
1 cup oat milk
1/2 cup water
2 tbsp pumpkin seeds
1 tsp salt
1 tsp yeast

Mix the pumpkin with the sage and 1 tbsp of oil. Bake in a oven at 200 degrees C for 20-25 minutes.
Mix the flour and seeds, add the liquids and yeast to form a dough. Roll out to fit a baking tray or pizza stone. Place dough onto the tray or stone, that has preferably been preheated first. Push the pumpkin onto the dough; mix the garlic into the remaining 1 tbsp oil and drizzle over the pumpkin. Bake in the oven for 15 minutes.

CAULIFLOWER "CHEESE"

Cauliflower is a great autumn vegetable; in this version of a classic dish, you use tofu instead of cheese for a fantastic vegan variation.

1 medium cauliflower
2 tbsp ground almonds
For the tofu cheese:
250g tofu
1 tbsp sweet miso
1 tbsp ume paste
1/2 tbsp mustard
1 tbsp tahini or nut butter
1 tbsp olive oil
4 tbsp water

Steam the whole cauliflower head for 10 minutes until al dente. Mix the seasonings together. Crumble the tofu and blend with the rest of the ingredients to make the 'cheese'. Spread over the steamed cauliflower and sprinkle ground almonds over the top. Bake in an oven preheated to 200 degrees C for 20 minutes or until golden on top.

A strong grain side dish, energy rich and nourishing as we go into the colder months. I use left over short grain brown rice cooked two part water to one part grain in a pressure cooker.

RICE AND SESAME CROQUETTES

Makes 12-14:
3 cups left over pressure cooked rice
1 tbsp sesame seeds
1 tbsp tahini
1/2 tbsp shoyu
1/2 l cooking oil

Mix together all the ingredients except the cooking oil.
Form into golf ball size rounds by firm pressure in your palm. Heat the oil in a pan, or a small wok if you have one. Fry the croquettes in 2-3 batches for 3-4 minutes each batch until golden and crispy. Serve with a tasty mustard dip.

A great short grain rice dish that uses the strong energy of this rice and a pressure cooker that are both brilliant for strengthening our Metal energy.

JERUSALEM ARTICHOKE RISOTTO

Serves 4-6:
2 cups rice
4-5 Jerusalem artichokes
2 sticks celery
2 small onions
1 tbsp fresh marjoram or thyme, chopped
2 cloves garlic
Seasonings:
1 tbsp mirin, 1 tbsp tahini
1 tbsp ume paste, 1 tbsp sweet miso

Dice and sauté the onion, celery and garlic for 10 minutes in the bottom of the pressure cooker pan. Add the rice and 4 cups water or stock. Bring to pressure and cook for 45 minutes. Mix together the seasoning ingredients. Remove from heat and once the pressure has come down, stir in the seasonings and herbs.

FRIED MACKEREL OR TEMPEH'

A lovely battered fish recipe. I stumbled across this way of making my batter when Triin was staying here for photo shoot. She is totally gluten free, so I needed to find a batter to suit. I used buckwheat flour which, to my delight, I discovered makes a fantastic batter. This is a hearty dish for autumn and winter warming.

Serves 4:
1/2 cup buckwheat flour
1/2 cup arrowroot
3/4 cup water
1 tsp salt
4 mackerel fillets or 1 pack of organic tempeh
1/2 sunflower oil
Shoyu for a dip

Prepare the fish by taking out the middle bone and cutting into pieces. If using tempeh, cut into bite size pieces. Mix the flour, arrowroot, salt and water together to form a smooth batter. Dip the fish or tempeh in the batter, coating each piece completely, and deep fry in batches in hot oil for 2-3 minutes or until golden.

MISO AND GINGER SOUP

I also call this 'Get-well-again Soup', as it's fantastic to help recovery from any illness. It's good in autumn and also supports the winter element of Water. It's a very flexible recipe and you can use whatever vege-tables you have available. The miso and wakame add nutrients and depth, the pungent ginger nourishes and clears the body of toxins.

Serves 4-6:
4 cups of hard veg diced:
carrot, onion, turnip, celery, swede.
1 cup cauliflower cut into florets
1 cup kale or other greens shredded
1 piece of wakame sea vegetable,
soaked and chopped in small pieces
6-7 cups water or stock
1 tbps ginger peeled and grated
1-2 tbsp miso, mixed into a runny
paste with some water

Saute the hard vegetables, in a little oil, with the ginger for about 5 minutes. Add the water and bring to the boil. Simmer for 10-15 minutes. Add cauliflower florets and wakame. Simmer until soft, adding greens last. Turn off and add miso. Garnish with chopped spring onion and/or garden herbs.
Serve immediately.

Light and creamy, yet wholesome and grounding, parsnips make a fabulous soup. This soup is great for Earth energy too, as it's lovely and sweet.

CREAMY PARSNIP SOUP

4-5 parsnips, cubed (about 4 cups)
1 onion, diced
1 tsp salt
1 tsp ground cumin
1 garlic clove
1 tbsp finely chopped ginger
4 cups stock or water
1 cup oat cream

Saute, in 1 tbsp oil, the onion, garlic, cumin, ginger and salt for 5 minutes. Add the parsnip and water. Simmer for 15-20 minutes until the vegetables are soft. Blend the soup, adding the cream. Serve warm, with parsley, toasted seeds and/or croutons.

ARAME PASTY

A vegan pasty great for autumn. All the health benefits of sea vegetables in a yummy baked dish; the kids love this one too. You can also use hiziki which suits the Metal element well. Making individual pasties similar to cornish pasties is really fun; sometimes, I add some crumbled tofu inside too to make a great lunch or tea for the children.

Makes 6-7 pasties:
For the filling:
1 tbsp apple concentrate
1 cup arame, soaked in 2 cups water
1 tbsp oil
1 large carrot grated, optional
1 onion, cut into half moons
2 tbsp shoyo
For the pastry
2 1/2 cups wholemeal flour
3 tbsp oil
1 tbsp poppy or flax seeds
2/3 cup water

Sauté the onions and carrots in the oil, with a pinch of salt, for 5-10 minutes. Add the arame and soaking water and cook for about 25 minutes. Season to taste with shoyu and apple concentrate, and cook until most of the liquid has evaporated. Mix the flour, oil and seeds, mix in the water to form a pastry; roll out and cut into circles. Add the filling in the middle and fold over the pasty to cover, pinching closed at the edges. Place them on a baking tray and cook in an oven preheated to 180 degrees C for 20 minutes or until golden.

Baked vegetables are nourishing and satisfying, and great for strengthening any meal, specially good in late autumn or winter. You can choose from any hard root or on the ground vegetables; my favourites to bake are parsnips, onions, beetroot, sweet potatoes, pumpkin, butternut squash.

ROASTED VEGETABLES

Serves 4-6:
4 cups hard vegetables cut into chunks 2-3cm
2 tbsp oil
1 tbsp shoyu

Chop the vegetables into even sized chunks, 2 or 3cm square. Rub in olive oil and bake in the oven at 180 degrees C for about 45-50 minutes, making sure you toss regularly to prevent burning. Sprinkle with a splash of shoyu and serve.

Kale is the King of the vegetables. It has an amazing amount of iron, calcium and other essential vitamins and minerals. I try to include some in my diet once a day. This recipe adds sesame seeds which gives even more calcium.

SAUTED KALE WITH GARLIC

Serves 4:
1 head kale, de stemmed and sliced in to strips.
1 spoon sesame seeds, toasted.
1 clove garlic finely sliced

Begin by frying the kale in a little oil. Add a splash of water and water saute for 2 minutes. Add the garlic and seeds and cook for a further 2 minutes until the kale is soft.

I love turnips, they are a traditional food that grows easily, and I think they are seriously under-rated. But I am a big fan... they go into my stews and soups and baked, they are delicious.

STEAMED TURNIP WITH UME VINEGAR

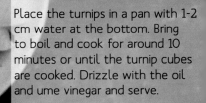

Serves 4:
4 medium turnips, cut into cubes
1 tbsp olive oil
1 tbsp ume vinegar

Place the turnips in a pan with 1-2 cm water at the bottom. Bring to boil and cook for around 10 minutes or until the turnip cubes are cooked. Drizzle with the oil and ume vinegar and serve.

This root vegetable collaboration creates a hearty side dish that is satisfying and tasty. Also, it can be used as an alternative to mash potatoes topping to any pie.

PARSNIP AND CELERIAC MASH

Serves 4-6:
1/2 large or one small celeriac, cut into 1inch cubes
2-3 parsnips, peeled and cut into 1inch cubes
2 tbsp olive oil
pinch of salt

Saute the vegetables in 1 tbsp oil for 5 minutes with a pinch of salt. Add 1 inch water and cook for 10 minutes until the vegetables are soft and the water has evaporated. Add the extra tbsp of oil and mash. I like it chunky but mash to your preferred texture and serve with fresh marjoram to garnish.

155

A really simple and effective recipe with no gluten dairy or sugar, just fruit and nut, how fantastic. This recipe makes about 12-14 pieces. If you want less, then halve it and use a loaf tin for baking.

FRUIT AND NUT SLICE

Serves 8-10 :
2 cups dried mixed vine fruit
1 cup dried apricots, chopped
2 cups chopped dates
2 cups water
2 cups ground almonds
1 cup walnuts or sunflower seeds
1 tsp cinnamon
1tsp nutmeg
1 tbsp lemon rind

Place dates and water in a small pan. Bring to boil and simmer for about 5 minutes until the dates are very soft, and mash to a smooth paste. Mix all the rest of ingredients together and then stir in the date mixture. Place the mixture in a 9" square loaf tin, and bake in a preheated oven at 160 degrees C for 45 minutes.

A beautiful desert using the sacred rosehip syrup for a light but satisfying completion to a meal.

ROSEHIP KANTEN

Makes 4-5:
2 cups water
3 tbps agar flakes
2 cup rosehip syrup (p.160)
Hazelnuts to garnish

Heat the agar in the water until it has dissolved, about 8 minutes. Add the syrup and then leave to set in a cool place. Toast some chopped hazelnuts and garnish to serve.

GINGER MUFFINS

Ginger has a fantastic energy that is deep and lively. These muffins are a yummy alternative to ginger biscuits and a great autumn treat, warm and strong from baking and alive from the energy of ginger.

Makes 10-12 muffins:
2 1/2 cups wholemeal flour
1 cup white flour
2" ginger root, peeled and grated
1 tbsp baking powder
1 tsp mixed spice
1/2 cup rice or oat milk
1/2 cup safflower or sunflower oil
1/2 cup barley malt
1/4 cup apple concentrate
1/4 cup rice syrup
Topping:
2 tbsp barley malt
1 tbsp boiling water

Heat oven to 170 degrees C. Sieve and mix the dry ingredients together. Mix the wet ingredients together, including the ginger. Mix wet and dry ingredients together. Fill muffin cases 3/4 full and bake in the oven for 20 minutes. Mix boiling water with extra barley malt and drizzle on top of the cooked muffins.

APPLE AND ALMOND CRUNCH

Apples are an early and late autumn gift. I love to cut them in half through the middle to find the hidden star inside. Here at Sunny Brow, we have a fabulous orchard with an array of trees with different apples of varying sizes, tastes and sweetness levels. You can use cooking or eating apples for this recipe. Add more sweetener to taste if your apple mixture is more sour than would you like.

4-5 large apples, peeled cored and
chopped into small chunks
1 tbsp almond butter
1-2 tbsp barley or rice syrup, depending on
your apple sweetness
for the crunch topping:
2 1/2 cups porridge oats
3/4 cup ground almonds
1/4 cup olive oil
3/4 cup rice syrup
1/2 tsp salt

Cook the apples in 2tbsp juice or water until soft, about 10-15 minutes. Stir in the almond butter and barley malt. Place in the bottom of an oven proof dish. Mix ingredients for the crunch together, and lay on top of the apples. Bake at 170 degrees C for 20-25 minutes or until golden brown and bubbling, very tasty served with oatly oat cream.

Rosehips feel so special, I find them a magical and sacred ingredient; I love to harvest them at this time of year and create a rosehip syrup that harnesses their energy. They are also incredibly high in vitamin C. This syrup can then be used in other recipes or enjoyed as a drink.

ROSEHIP SYRUP

3 cups wild rosehips
4-5 cups water
1 1/2 cups apple concentrate

Begin by bringing the rosehips to boil in 4 cups of water; if you want to halve them first, this can help but it's not essential if time is an issue. Simmer for about an hour. Blend or mash the hips in the water; add 1-2 cups more water and simmer again for another hour. Remove from heat and add the apple concentrate. Strain into a jug and transfer to your chosen container; refrigerate and it will keep for several days.

BLACKBERRY AND HAZELNUT SLICE

A recipe idea from my son Roan when he was 5; it was created as we were out picking blackberries and he noticed the hazelnuts were ready too, the idea of blackberries and hazelnuts in a flapjack caused great excitement.

Serves 6-8:
2 cup porridge oats
1 cup jumbo oats
1 cup hazelnuts, chopped and toasted
1/2 cup olive oil
1 1/2 cups wild blackberries
3/4 cup rice syrup

Heat the oven to 170 degrees C.
Mix all ingredients together and bake in a 9"square tin for 25-30 minutes.
Well done Roan - very yummy.

It's not a quick job to make a batch of this coffee but well worth the while. Make sure you dig up the roots whilst you can still see the leaves so you know where to look.

DANDELION ROOT COFFEE

Step 1: Dig up a handful of dandelion roots. I get about 4-5 large roots.
Step 2: Scrub them clean and chop roughly into chunks.
Step 3: Grind the roots in a food processor until in small pieces.
Step 4: Bake in the oven at 100 degrees C for about 30-60 minutes until dried and dark golden brown.
Step 5: Cool and store in a glass jar.

To make a coffee, use 1 tbsp and toast over a flame to bring out more flavour. Then add 3 cups water and bring to the boil. Simmer for 5 minutes. And serve black or white with oat milk. A delicious wild drink with the strong energy of roots.

A great bread, although it's very much like a cake too. So a good blend of cake and bread, with nutrition benefits and flavours from walnuts and bananas, that makes an enjoyable autumnal afternoon tea.

BANANA AND WALNUT BREAD

2 1/2 cups wholemeal spelt flour
1 cup white flour
1 cup walnuts, chopped
1 heaped tbsp baking powder
2 large ripe bananas
1 cup oat milk
1/2 cup water
2 tbsp rice syrup

Blend the bananas with the milk, water and syrup. Mix the flours, nuts and baking powder and mix with the blended banana and milk. Place the thick batter into a lined loaf tin; cook in the oven for 1 hour at 150 degrees C.

ROSEHIP AND YARROW INFUSION

Full of the health benefits of rosehip and yarrow with a beautiful delicate and enjoyable balanced flavour. This is a perfect healing yet tasty drink for the autumn, with the yarrow complimenting the sweeter rosehips.

Serves 2:
2 cups water
12 rosehips
1-2 yarrow flower heads and leaves

Halve and simmer the rosehips for 10 minutes.
Add the yarrow and infuse for 5 minutes.

GINGER AND LEMON INFUSION

Lemon and ginger make a great team, this tea is lovely in Autumn to stay light but nourished too. No need to use a peeler either, you can use the whole of the ginger and lemon.

Serves 2-3:
1 tbsp grated ginger
2 slices of lemon
2-3 cups boiling water
Rice syrup to taste (optional)

Place the ginger and lemon in a tea pot and pour over the boiling water. Allow to steep for 5 minutes. Serve with sweetener to suit individual taste if desired.

WINTER

AND THE ELEMENT OF WATER

Winter is here and life outside is dormant. The weather gets colder and can be severe at times. Here at Sunny Brow, we can really feel the elements with the strong energies of wind, rain, ice and snow, reminding us of their power. The trees and many animals are in hibernation. Support in this season feels essential; it can feel like a long wait until spring and the shoots of new life. We snuggle up in front of the fire, and gather indoors with friends and family. The darkest time of year draws us to internally reflect. Although there is no outer growth in the natural world, the energy is still within the roots. Using winter to nourish our own roots can give us a stronger foundation in life. Personally, I find the more I honour the energy of this time of year, the easier the winter is. I draw more inward and enjoy quieter evenings nurturing and working on new projects and ideas, rather than rushing out in action. With a conscious and positive contraction, it allows me to stay soft and open, and keeps away any winter blues.

Christmas and Winter Solstice festivities are treasures at this time of year, serving to bring us together and help us through the winter months. Candles and fairy lights of Christmas can warm the heart and bring light to the dark. The Winter Solstice, on or around the 21st December, is a great marker point where the dark is at its height, but it is actually the transition into the light coming. It is a perfect time to pause and assess ourselves, view the year and integrate it all before the cycle starts over again.

The food in this season is supportive for the darkness and colder months. Any foods rich in minerals and vitamins can be vital at this time of year. The cold weather and dark energy can deplete our reserves, so it's good to keep them topped up with quality mineral rich foods, fish, stews, perhaps some wild meats, root vegetables, buckwheat and heaps of winter greens. The array of root vegetables from autumn can roll into winter. Stews and soups have a fantastic grounding, softening energy and using good vegetables, cut into a chunky style, and slow cooked, we can gently support and nourish our roots.

In season are brussels, celery, winter greens and cabbages, cauliflower, celeriac, jerusalem artichokes, burdock or salsify root, kale, leeks, swede, parsnips, carrots, chestnuts and red cabbage.

From an 'in the wild' perspective, nature does not provide too much at this time of year. The things available are very limited. Here at Sunny Brow, I mainly find wintercress, a peppery rocket like leaf, which I add to winter salads. And then, of course, winter is an appropriate time of year to hunt for wild game. I have included a recipe of wild venison, as this is something we have here at Sunny Brow. I don't personally eat a lot of meat, but if I do, quality meats from animals that have had a quality life, and that are killed and eaten with gratitude, is my only choice.

The element related to this time of year in the oriental system is Water. The corresponding organs are kidney and bladder. Water is essential to life, it is this essence that helps to understand this energy and how it relates to winter. The winter season and Water element is linked to both life beginning, in the womb, and to death, the return source. Water is the element connected to the sacral chakra and, therefore, womb in women. It is existence and non existence. When I connect to the element of water, I always sense its energy of giving and taking life. It is a deep and profound element. If we have strength with our Water, we will have courage; if it is imbalanced, fear will begin to dominate. If we fear life and death, if we don't understand our truth or comprehend the essence of life and death, we will feel fear. Fear freezes us and can damage our Water energy. In Winter, we need to conserve and preserve our 'essence' and our potential. This is a time for storage of our potential energy, and of rest and repair. The Water element is about rest and passivity, which is an important part of the cycle as is the cold to balance hot. However, in colder months, we are more easily depleted, with less warmth and light to support us, so we must be more careful. As Water is our 'essence', this element can easily become imbalanced. We can always do with more 'essence' in our lives, so excess is rare. Our focus should be how to increase and support Water. People with an imbalance in their Water energy will struggle more in winter; excessive tiredness, insomnia, anxiety or overriding fear, or the feeling where the cold hits deep into the bones are all signs of an imbalance in 'Water' energy. Warming foods, and nourishment from vitamins and minerals are the key to this season. I always include more fish in our diet at this time of year. For vegans, it recommended to be especially careful and aware to make sure you top up with enough minerals with quality vegetables, sea vegetables and condiments using sesame and pumpkin seeds.

Although water itself is essential to wellbeing, it is also not good to flush excessive amounts of water through our kidneys, especially in the winter, as this can potentially weaken them. One way to enjoy water at this time of year is from broths, teas and soups. In this way, we are not cooling the system or risking depleting reserves and straining the kidneys and bladder. In our culture, maybe, we need more water to flush out bad foods and alcohol, but once we begin eating a clean diet, rich in vegetables, soups and healthy proteins, the need for excessive water reduces.

Salt is the flavour to support 'Water'; make sure you are using good quality salts, shoyu, miso and sea vegetables. Too much salt though, especially if it's bad quality will actually do more harm than good. It's a good idea to work intuitively with salt intake and experiment with what feels right for you. Dark scanty urine may indicate that you are taking too much, clear excessive urine and you are possibly not getting enough. Support from the previous element, Metal, can help in winter, so foods in the previous chapter are also good. One of the main things to be very aware of is the impact of Fire element foods. In winter, be especially careful of overly excessive sweet things, too many spices and raw foods, as these can weaken the blood and rob our reserves. It's good to try to choose gentle sweetness to allow relaxation rather than depletion.

Cooking to support our Water energy:
Buckwheat, small dark beans (black and aduki), steamed winter greens, fish or small quantities of quality meats, salty flavour, miso and quality salts, burdock or salsify, condiments made with seeds, soups, stews and broths, chunky cut vegetables, long slow cooking, sea vegetables.

Warming foods to support in Winter:
Ginger, mustard, winter herbs rosemary and sage, turnip and root vegetables, walnuts and other nuts, lamb and game, prawns, nutmeg and cinnamon.

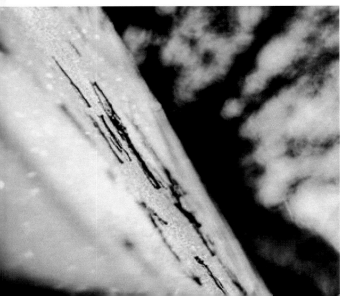

169

A winter warmer that makes a satisfying meal when served with a wholegrain, such as buckwheat, and some steamed greens. I also make this dish sometimes adding fried seitan, tofu or a hearty bean such as butterbean. You can use whichever winter roots you have available.

ROOT VEGETABLES
WITH MISO AND WHOLEGRAIN MUSTARD

1 stick salsify or burdock
1 large carrot
1 large parsnip
1 onion
2 sticks celery
1 cup swede
1 cup celeriac
2-3 cups water
2 bay leaves
1heaped tbsp arrowroot, made into paste with a little water.
Seasonings: 1-2 tbsp barley miso, 1 spoon of wholegrain mustard.

Cut the vegetables into similar shaped chunks. Saute them in a large pan with 1 tbsp oil; add 2-3 cups water, and then add the bay leaves. When boiling, turn down to low and simmer for 20 minutes or until the vegetables are soft. Add arrowroot and stir to thicken. Stir in the seasonings and serve.

BUCKWHEAT AND SEED BURGERS

Buckwheat is gluten free, hearty and energising, perfect winter food. These burgers are tasty and nutritious. As we are lucky enough to have our own chickens, I use an egg in this recipe to bind the burgers. If you don't have a good source of eggs, or are vegan, then the recipe works equally well without an egg; however, make sure to include flax seeds in your seed mix as these help the binding.

1 cup buckwheat
2 cups water
1 cup mixed seeds, toasted and ground
1 onion, diced small
1 carrot, grated
1 tsp mixed herbs
garlic, chopped finely
1 egg (optional)
2 tbsp buckwheat flour
oil for frying.

Toast the buckwheat until it smells nutty, be careful not to burn, it serves to bring out the lovely flavour. Add the water, bring to the boil, and then cover and turn the heat to low until all the water is absorbed, and the buckwheat is soft, about 20 minutes. Meanwhile, saute the onion, carrot, garlic and herbs until soft. Mix all the ingredients together and make into small burger shapes. Fry in batches with 2 tbsp sesame oil per batch until golden brown on both sides, approximately 3-4 minutes.

This is my interpretation of traditional Japanese dish that is served quite ceremonially in the middle of the table with everyone helping themselves from the middle pot. I learnt about this dish on my macrobiotic training, it beautifully supports the Water element. When I eat this dish, I feel incredibly nourished on every level. It's a real treat. I choose to serve it in individual bowls, with extra dipping sauce for people to add to their taste. If you are vegan, do not rule out this dish, as you can replace the fish with some tofu chunks or seitan.

SUNNY BROW NABE

Serves 4:
1 large carrot
1/2 small butternut squash
1-2 heads pak choi
1-2 leeks
1 small head of broccoli
12 muscles
8-12 large prawns
1 fillet of white fish chunks
4" piece of kelp/kombu
1 x packet of semi buckwheat noodles, cooked until al dente
For the seasoning sauce:
8 dried shitake mushrooms, soaked in a cup of water
2 spring onions, diced small
1 tbsp sesame seeds, toasted
1/4 cup shoyu
2 inch ginger, grated and squeezed for juice

Begin by making a kombu dashi by boiling the kombu in a large pan with 2 litres of water for approximately 30 minutes. Cut the vegetables into long thin slices or chunks, and blanch each individual type of vegetable in the Kombu dashi, removing and refreshing when soft to prevent over cooking. Make the sauce by slicing the mushrooms and adding the shoyu to the mushrooms and 1/2 cup of the mushroom liquid. Add the toasted seeds and the remaining ingredients. Last thing to cook is the fish and seafood, this can be added to the hot broth at the end and allow to simmer for a few minutes until the fish has cooked through. Add the vegetables back to the pan and heat through. To complete the dish, add the noodles into individual bowls and pour the hot broth and cooked fish and vegetables into the bowls; add the sauce to taste and serve.

This was actually partly my husband's creation, so some credit to him too here. It is very Italian in influence and is a winner with all the family. I feel happy that the children are getting their omega 3 for good brain power, and with secret vegetables too, it's an all round hit. I was taught this technique of adding the pasta to the sauce by a lovely Italian chef; it's a great tip that makes for flavoursome pasta dishes.

SARDINE PASTA

Serves 4-6:
2 tins sardines in oil
1 large onion, diced small
1 carrot grated or small matchsticks
1 tin tomatoes
1 tbsp balsamic vinegar
300g wholemeal penne
1 tbsp of shoyu
1 tbsp chopped parsley or basil

Saute the onion and carrots with 1 tsp salt in 1 tbsp olive oil to bring out their sweetness. The longer you saute here, the tastier the dish, just be careful not to burn, 10-15 minutes is good.
While you are cooking the vegetables, open the sardines and drain the oil into the pan with onions and carrots. Remove the middle bones from the sardines and chop into rough pieces; add them to the vegetables, with the tomatoes, balsamic vinegar and 1 cup of water. Simmer the sauce for 30-45minutes, making sure it does not go too dry, add more water if needed. Season with shoyu. Cook the pasta until 3/4 cooked, then drain, reserving 1 cup of the water. Add the pasta into the sardine sauce with the cup of cooking liquid, and complete the cooking of the pasta in the sauce. Add some parsley or basil and serve immediately.

Another great winter warmer and using the sweet and nutty aduki bean gives a hearty, nutritious and tasty meal. As with the fish pie, you can juggle the toppings for just millet or just potato but I really like this combo of both. You can play around with the inside of the pie too, adding squash for extra sweetness and Earth energy.

RED DRAGON PIE

Serves 6-8:
2 cups aduki beans, soaked in 6 cups water
1 large onion, diced
1 large carrot, diced
1-2 sticks celery, diced
1 clove garlic, cut finely
2 tsp mixed herbs
1/2 squash, cut into small chunks (optional)
1 tin tomatoes (or 1 cup no 'tomato' sauce p.186.)
Seasonings: 2 tbsp shoyu and 1 tbsp apple concentrate
1 1/2 cup millet
4-5 small potatoes, cut into small chunks
4 cups water
2-3 tbsp olive oi

Cook the aduki beans by bringing them to the boil in their soaking water, skim off any froth from the top, and add a piece of kombu sea vegetable. Cover and turn to a simmer, and cook gently for approx 45 minutes. Saute the onions, carrot and celery in a little olive oil for 5 minutes; add a pinch of salt, the garlic and the mixed herbs, and saute for a further 5 minutes. Add this mixture to the beans, with the tomato and squash if you are using. Cook the whole mixture for another 25 minutes, adding a little more water if it gets too dry. Add the seasonings and place in an oven proof dish. As the beans are cooking, in another large pan, toast the millet grain, add the water, potatoes and salt, and bring to the boil. Turn down to very low, cover with a lid, place on a flame spreader and cook for 20-25 minutes or until all the water is absorbed and the millet and potatoes are soft. Add the olive oil and mash until smooth.
Cover the bean mixture with the millet and potato mash, and bake in a hot oven (200 degrees C) for 25 minutes, or until golden and bubbling.

FISH AND MILLET PIE

This is one of my favourite dishes. I just love the warmth, satisfaction and nourishment it provides. We serve it with peas and/or greens for a perfect winter meal. The topping can be swapped for the other topping for red dragon pie, or just a simpler potato one. I juggle them around depending on how I'm feeling. The millet gives stronger, richer dish than potato.

Serves 6-8:
6-8 fillets of fish, salmon, cod,
haddock, skinned and cut into chunks
1 carrot, diced small
1 onion, diced small
Pinch of salt
3/4 cup oat or other vegan cream
1 tsp mustard
1 tbsp white miso
1 tbsp ume puree
2 cups millet
5 cups water
2-3 tbsp olive oil
1 tsp salt

In a large pan, toast the millet grain. This brings out a lovely nutty flavour. Add the water and bring to the boil, then add the salt. Turn down to very low and place on a flame spreader if you have one; cover, and cook for 20-25 mins or until all the water is absorbed. When cooked, add the olive oil and mix until combined. Whilst the millet is cooking, saute the onion and carrot with the pinch of salt in a little oil until they are soft. The salt brings out the sweetness. Mix together the cream and seasonings until smooth and add to the vegetables. Add the fish and place in a oven dish. Cover with the millet and bake for 25 minutes, or until golden and bubbling, in an oven heated to 200C.

A very wholesome and relaxing soup based on the classic macrobiotic dish 'aduki beans and squash', which is a healing dish for kidney and bladder, and our Water energy.

ADUKI AND BUTTERNUT SQUASH SOUP

Serves 4-6:
1 large butternut squash, cubed
1 cup cooked Aduki beans, preferably home cooked with kombu
1 onion, diced
4 cups water
1-2 tbsp shoyu or tamari soy sauce

Saute the onion for 5 minutes in 1 tbsp olive oil and a pinch of salt; add squash and saute on a low heat for 5 minutes. Add the water and beans and simmer for 20 minutes. Season with the soy sauce 5 minutes from the end of cooking. Blend the soup until smooth, or part blend for a more textured variation. Serve, garnished with parsley.

WINTER VEGETABLE SOUP WITH CROUTONS

This is warming, easy to create and is very flexible around what you have in the vegetables store, what arrived in your vegetable box or your seasonal favourites. Root vegetables cooked in a soup are so nourishing in winter.

Serves 4-6:
1 large carrot
1/2 swede
1/2 cabbage
1/2 small squash (about 1 cup)
1 parsnip
2 sticks celery
1 onion
1-2 cloves garlic
1 piece wakame
1 tbsp bouillon
6 cups water
1 cup oat cream
For the croutons:
2 thick slices of granary bread
2 tbsp oil

Cut all the vegetables into chunks. Saute the onion, carrot and celery for 5 minutes. Add the rest of the vegetables and garlic and cook for a further 5 minutes. Add water, wakame and bouillon, bring to boil, and then turn to low heat, simmering for 20 minutes. Blend, adding the oat cream.

For the croutons:
Cut two thick slices of homemade bread and cut into squares. Heat the oil and fry croutons for about 5 minutes, until crispy. Serve on top of the soup.

NUT LOAF

A super alternative for a roast dinner, nutritious and healthy, and very flexible. You can use whatever nuts or seeds in the loaf that you like and can add left over grains too. I like to serve this with an onion gravy or a no 'tomato sauce', p.186, and plenty of steamed and roasted vegetables.

2 sticks celery, diced
1 onion
1 carrot
1 tsp mixed herbs
2 tbsp oil
1/2 tsp salt
1 1/2 cups nuts, toasted and ground
1 cup cooked chesnuts
1 cup bread crumbs or cooked
millet or short grain brown rice
1 egg, optional
2 garlic clove

Saute the vegetables and garlic with the salt and oil, on a low flame, for about 15 minutes. The veg will soften and sweeten. Add to the ground nuts. If using breadcrumbs, add 2 tbsp of water to soften. Add crumbs or grain to the loaf. Adding an egg will help the mixture to bind but its not essential if you are vegan. Press into a lined loaf tin and bake at 180 degrees C for 35-40 minutes.

WINTER STEW WITH JUNIPER

Venison and junipers are a classic combination, adding barley and root vegetables and slow cooking produces a great stew. When cooking meat, I honour and thank the animal for its give away. With wild meats, we can pretty much know that the animal has had a good life, no hormones or too much stress from environment. If we are going to eat meat, this is the healthiest way. For vegans, this stew can work well with fried seitan.

600g wild venison meat, diced
or 2 cups sliced seitan
1/2 cup barley grain
1-2 cloves garlic, diced finely
1 tsp juniper berries, crushed
1 large onion, cut into chunks
1 large carrot, cut into chunks
2 bay leaves
1 tbsp dijon mustard
Salt and pepper
2-3 tbsp olive oil
1 tbsp apple cider vingar
1/2 cup apricots

Heat the oven to 150 degrees C
Marinate the meat, overnight if possible, with the garlic, mustard, seasonings, olive oil, junipers and apple cider vinegar. Fry the meat or seitan on a high flame to brown. Place in an oven proof stew pot and add the remaining ingredients. Cover with water or homemade stock to just the top of the ingredients. Cook for 2-2 1/2 hours until the sauce is thickened.

1 - Place in a large bowl and cover with water and leave overnight. (Or cover in warm water and soak for 1-2 hours.) Then begin to wash and knead in water.

2 - Mix water and flour until a dough is formed. Knead the dough for 5-15 minutes. The more you knead, the better, but if time is short, then 5 mins is OK.

3 - Finish the rinsing with a cold water rinse to contract the seitan. Form into about 5-6 chunks.

4 - Wash the dough throughly, alternating with hot and cold water. The starch will wash out in the water, refresh and drain several times until the water runs clear, this takes about 15-20 minutes.

5 - Put a pan of about 7 cups water to boil. Add the seitan and cook for 5 minutes. Add the shoyu, kombu and ginger, turn flame to low, and cook for about an hour.

6 - These are the finished seitan chunks. To fry, slice into thin strips and coat in arrowroot. Shallow fry on medium heat until crispy and serve with a dip.

STEP BY STEP: SEITAN

Seitan is a highly nutritious vegetarian protein made from wheat flour. The process involves removing the starch from the flour, which leaves you with the protein, gluten, from the wheat. Those I know with sensitivity to gluten in baked flour products do seem able to enjoy seitan, so don't let the gluten word put you off. This protein is very tasty, versatile and has more protein per gram that beef. It's pretty straight forward and very satisfying to make once you get a few key points right. The main one being the type of flour. It needs to be very strong flour. Once you've got the technique, you have an inexpensive and tasty vegan protein, blended it makes a great mince substitute. This batch will normally produce two decent seitan meals for a family/ group of 4-6.

1 x 2.5 kg bag of very strong white flour
7 cups water
to cook:
1 6" piece kombu
1/2 cup shoyu
Ginger slices (optional)
To fry:
2 tbsp arrowroot
Sesame or olive oil

SEITAN "MEAT" BALLS

Once you have your seitan, you are ready to transform it into some yummy dishes. It acts fairly similar to meat and can be used as a substitute in many recipes. This 'meat' ball recipe includes seeds to make a protein, calcium and iron rich dish. If you haven't got time to make your seitan, then it can be bought in, although of course, it's preferable to use your own. I serve this dish with a nice gravy or no tomato sauce and lots of vegetables.

Makes 22-24:
2 cups seitan, blended to a mince
1 cup sunflower seeds, toasted
and ground
1 onion, diced finely
1 clove garlic, finely chopped
1 tsp salt
1 tbsp parsley chopped finely
2 tbsp buckwheat flour
1 tbsp shoyu
Oil for frying

Saute the onion with the salt in 1 tbsp oil. Add the garlic and fry until they are both soft. Add the minced seitan and fry for 5 more minutes, then mix or blend quickly to combine. Mix all the ingredients together in a large bowl. Make into even sized balls, about the size of a golf ball. Shallow fry evenly on a medium heat for 5 minutes, turning frequently. I normally do this in 2-3 batches, using 1 tbsp olive oil per batch.

BLACK BEANS

Black beans are supportive in winter months, dark, mysterious and nutritious, sweet and yummy. High in phyto nutrients, B6 and potassium and with properties to reduce cholesterol, and maintain a healthy digestive track; it is hard to think why we would not include these in our diet. This recipe can be a soup or a stew. Just adjust the water you need for both these options. I often make a stew and then add more water or stock the next day to enjoy as a soup.

2 cups black beans
6 - 8 cups water
1 piece kombu
1 large onion
2 tsp cumin
1 tsp salt
2 cloves garlic, finely chopped
Seasonings:
1 tbsp apple concentrate
2 tbsp shoyu
2 tbsp fresh coriander, chopped

Soak the black beans with the kombu in the water; 6 cups for a stew or 8 cups for a soup. Soak for 6-8 hours or over night. To cook the beans, bring them to the boil, skim off any froth that has been created, cover and turn down to simmer for about 40 minutes. Meanwhile, saute the onion, cumin, salt and garlic in a little oil, until soft. Add into the beans and continue cooking for another 10-20 minutes. Add the seasonings to taste 5 minutes before the end of cooking. To complete, stir in the coriander and allow to infuse.

Hearty, sweet and satisfying, roasting beetroot gives a great side dish to compliment any meal. I like the combination of sweet roasted beets and a pungent mustard dressing.

ROASTED BEETROOT

2-4 beetroots scrubbed and chopped into even chunks
1-2 tbsp olive oil
Dressing:
1 tsp dijon mustard
1 tbsp sweet miso
2 tbsp apple concentrate
1-2 tbsp apple cider vinegar
1 tsp ume vinegar

Rub the oil into the beetroot; place in a baking tray and bake in a preheated oven at 180 degrees C. Bake in the oven until soft, approx 45-55 minutes, depending on the size of your chunks, turning regularly. Serve with mustard dressing.

BRUSSELS WITH RED ONION AND WALNUTS

A great dish for when brussels come into season and tasty enough to serve at Christmas.

Serves 4-6:
4 cups brussel sprouts
1/2 red onion, diced small
1/2 tbsp freshly chopped sage
1/2 cup walnuts, chopped
1 tbsp olive, sesame or walnut oil
1 tsp salt

In a large frying pan, saute the onion with the oil and salt for 10 minutes, add the sage and walnuts and cook for a further couple of minutes. Steam the brussels for about 10 minutes until they are soft. Add the brussels into the pan with the onion mix and stir to combine.

This dish is a perfect balance of uplifting energy and good nutrition from the array of vegetables and the dulse. The tahini dressing adds some great minerals too. I have listed here the vegetables that I like to use, but you can add your own favourites; anything that can be blanched and crunchy is good.

WINTER VEGETABLE SALAD

1 large carrot
1/2 small swede
1/2 white cabbage
1 small head of broccoli
1/2 daikon/mooli
1/2 cup dulse, soaked til soft
and sliced thin

Cut the vegetables into interesting pieces that fit together in size and shape, diagonal half moons, or large matchsticks work well. Boil a pan of water and individually, blanch each set of vegetables until they are al dente, refreshing under cold water as soon as they are cooked. Combine all the cooked vegetables together with the dulse and serve, topped with toasted seeds and the tahini dressing from p67

Light and opening yet full of nutrients, a lovely side dish, that's actually great all year. The ume and oil set the vegetables off perfectly.

STEAMED KALE AND LEEK

Serves 3-4:
1 head kale, sliced
2 leeks, cut into 1" rounds
1/2-1 tbsp ume seasoning
1 tbsp olive oil

Place the leeks in the bottom of a pan and lay the kale in top. Add 1-2 cm of water and steam the vegetables for about 5-7 minutes. Drizzle over the ume seasoning and olive oil, stir and serve.

Gomasio is an amazing condiment made with sesame (goma) and salt (shio). It is full of calcium and other essential minerals. You can use it on any meal as a seasoning to enhance flavour and add nutition, We have it every day on our porridge, it's a vital part of our diet. The best thing to use for grinding is a Japanese suribachi which is like a pestle and mortor but with ridges in the mortor to aid the grinding. Be careful not to over grind, as you will get tahini. The key thing with gomasio is the salt and sesame ratio. Anything from 16:1 to 5:1 for a stronger energy; for my family, I go for about 16 or 14:1, as for me, it's mostly about the goodness of the sesame.

GOMASIO

14 tsp (1/4 cup) sesame seeds
1 tsp salt

Toast the seeds on a low until popping and fragrant, about 4-5 mintues. Add the salt. Put into the suribachi and grind in a spiral motion up and down to form the condiment, this should take about 2-3 minutes.

This is a fabulous replacement for a tomato sauce for pasta or pizza dishes. Tomatoes are a nightshade vegetable that can aggravate some symptoms like arthritis. I eat them in moderation so value this recipe and use it in the winter months when tomatoes definitely aren't in season.

NO 'TOMATO' SAUCE

1 cup grated carrot
1 cup grated squash
1 large onion, sliced finely
1/4 cup grated beetroot
1 tsp salt
1 cup water
1 tbsp olive oil

Saute the vegetables in the oil. Add the water and cook for 30 minutes. Blend until smooth.

WAKAME AND PUMPKIN SEED

This is a very tasty variation to gomasio that uses wakame instead of salt. It's rich in iron and calcium and is a great compliment to any meal.

1/2 cup wakame
1/2 cup pumpkin seeds

Place the wakame in the oven at 180 degrees C for 5 minutes, then grind in the suribachi. Toast the seeds until slightly browned to bring out the flavour, about 5 minutes. Grind the seeds until fine adding the wakame towards the end to combine.

Making a nice stock is very easy and can be made with any combination of vegetable cuts and peelings. Add whatever you have into a pan, with a piece of kombu; my son enjoys chopping it all up and this can make it super tasty but if you don't have an enthusiastic chopper, it's fine as it comes.

VEGETABLE AND KOMBU STOCK

1 6" piece kombu
1-2 cups vegetable and herb cuttings/peel
8 cups water

Bring all the ingredients to the boil and simmer for about 1/2 hour-1 hour. Strain and use in soups and stews.

MIXED WHOLEGRAIN PORRIDGE

This is an essential staple in our house, especially during the winter months. Whole grains have a great energy and are full of minerals, it is surprising to know that whole grains are a good source of iron and B vitamins. This porridge is a great way to get them into your and your family's diet. Grains are acidic, so adding a pinch of salt or kombu is important to help balance by adding some alkaline. I like to cook this in the evening. In the morning, I can then simply re-heat, adding cinnamon, nutmeg and raisins; serve, topped with seeds for a nutritious breakfast.

Serves 6-8:
2 cups wholegrains, I use a combination
of oat groats, millet, barley
and short grain brown rice.
10 cups filtered water
1 tsp salt or a piece of kombu/kelp

Place the grains and water in a large pan. You will need 5 times the amount of water to grain so 2 cups grain = 10 cups water. Bring the water and grains to the boil. Add the kombu. Turn down to a very low heat, using a flame spreader if you have one and simmer for about 1 1/2-2 hours until all the water has absorbed. Stir occasionally to prevent grains sticking and burning, this will also add creaminess.

Bread baking is great fun and very simple once you get going. Where I live, it's easier to bake a loaf than run to the shops and get a loaf. Plus, it's 10 times tastier and without any of the preservatives in shop bought bread that always concerns me. Homemade bread need not take forever, Sometimes, when I am short of time, I don't knead or rise the bread at all and still get a great loaf! Saying that the longer you give to it, the fluffier the loaf!

SUNNY BROW
SEEDED BREAD

7 cups wholemeal spelt flour
1 cup mixed seeds
1 tbsp barley malt
1 tsp salt
1 cup boiling water
1 cup oat milk
1/2 cup cold water
3 tsp yeast

Mix the dry ingredients together. Pour the boiling water over the barley malt and salt, stirring to combine. Add the rest of the wet ingredients and place the yeast on the top of these liquids. Mix together the wet and dry ingredients into a dough and knead for 5-10 minutes. Leave in a warm place for about 30 minutes. Knead back into a firm dough and place in a loaf tin. Bake for 50-60 minutes in an oven preheated to 150 degrees C. Remove from tin as soon as it's cooked and allow to cool on a wire rack.

CHESTNUT MOUSSE

Chestnuts are a great way to create a sweet desert that will not deplete our energy in winter, as chestnuts are highly nutritious, and due to being lovely and sweet, they don't need excessive sweetener to make them a satisfying desert.

1 cup amazake
1 cup oatmilk
1 cup chestnuts
Pinch of salt
2 tbsp rice malt syrup
1/4 tsp nutmeg
1 tbsp kuzu and 1 tbsp arrowroot,
diluted in a little water

Blend the milk, amazake and chestnuts until smooth. Place in a small pan, adding the nutmeg and salt Bring to a simmer and cook for 5 minutes. Add the kuzu and stir well, cooking for a couple more minutes. Lastly, add the syrup to your desired sweetness. Pour into small cups and serve, topped with toasted nuts or seeds.

NUTTY RICE PUDDING

A hearty desert full of goodness; a real nourishing winter warmer. I like to use leftover short grain brown rice, but any rice can work, so don't rule out any other leftovers.

2 cups leftover short or medium
grain brown rice
3 cups rice or oat milk
1/2 tsp nutmeg
1 tsp cinnamon
1 tbsp hazelnut/almond butter
1 tbsp chopped and toasted nuts
1-2 tbsp rice syrup

Add the rice, spices and milk to a pan and bring to simmer. Cook for about 1/2 hour on a very low heat until the mixture is thick and creamy. Add the syrup and nut butter to taste. Serve warm or chill and enjoy cold. Top with the toasted nuts to serve.

A winter treat; quite sweet for the Water element but a far better choice at Christmas to replace excessively sugary after dinner liqueurs and chocolates. These are very tasty made a day early to allow flavours to combine.

CHOCOLATE TRUFFLES

Makes about 25 truffles:
1 cup dried dates, chopped small
8 dried apricots, chopped small
1/2 cup boiling water
1/2 cup cocoa powder
1/2 cup desiccated coconut
2 tbsp ground almond
1 heaped tbsp coconut oil
2 tsp vanilla extract

Truffle coatings:
1 tbsp cocoa powder
2 tbsp desiccated coconut

Cover dates and apricot with the boiling water and leave for 10 minutes to soften. Place in a blender and add all the remaining ingredients, blend until combined. Form into small rounds and roll in truffle coatings. I like to do half the mixture in coconut and half in cocoa powder; refrigerate for at least 1 hour and serve.

This recipe is my version of sticky toffee pudding which is a lakeland classic. Creating a sugar free version using dates means we can enjoy the warm sticky yumminess here at Sunny Brow too.

STICKY DATE PUDDING

2 1/2 cups dates, chopped small
1 1/2 cups water
1/2 tsp salt
1 tbsp baking powder
2 1/2 cups wholemeal spelt flour
1/3 cup oil
2 tbsp barley malt
For the sauce:
3 tbsp rice malt syrup
2 tbsp pear and apple spread
1/2 cup water
1 tbsp kuzu or arrow root, diluted in a little water

Mix all the cake ingredients together. Place in a large pudding basin and cover with baking paper, using a length of string to fasten it to the basin. Place the pudding basin in a large saucepan with a couple of inches of water in the bottom. Place a tight lid on the pan and steam the pudding for 1 hour. For the sauce, heat all the ingredients and stir for about 2-3 minutes until thickened. To serve, place the pudding in individual bowls and pour over the sauce.

CHAI TEA

Warming and comforting; chai tea is a winner every time. For this winter version, I have avoided caffeine and spices that could deplete the body, using only those that warm and nourish in the colder months. I use barley malt to sweeten but rice syrup or other types work too.

Serves 4:
1" piece of ginger, sliced finely
Half stick cinnamon
1 small slice of nutmeg
1 star anise
2-3 cloves
3 cups water
2 tbsp barley malt

Place the ingredients in a small pan. You can keep the spices whole or crumble a little to allow flavours to infuse well. Simmer with a lid for 20 minutes. Add the sweetener. Strain and serve. Optional is to add some warmed oat milk for a creamier variation.

A healing tea for our Water energy; it's really great for the female system too. You can use the leftover beans from this drink in a soup or stew.

BLACK BEAN TEA

Serves 2:
1 cup black beans
5 cups water
2-3" piece kombu

Place all the ingredients in a pan and bring to the boil. Skim off any froth. Cover and cook on a low heat for 40-60 minutes. Strain the beans from the water, which will be dark and thicker, and serve.

INDEX

A to Z of ingredients

K